LOUIS NOWRA was born in Melbourne. He is the author of such plays as *Inner Voices, Visions, Inside the Island, The Precious Woman, Sunrise, The Golden Age, Capricornia, Byzantine Flowers, The Watchtower, Summer of the Aliens, Cosi, Radiance, The Temple, Crow, Miss Bosnia, The Incorruptible, The Jungle* and *The Language of the Gods*. He has written a non-fiction work *The Cheated*, three novels *The Misery of Beauty, Palu, Red Nights* and a memoir *The Twelfth of Never*. Some of his radio plays include *The Song Room, The Widows, Sydney, Moon of the Exploding Trees* and *The Divine Hammer*. Besides translating such plays as *The Prince of Homburg, Cyrano de Bergerac* and *Lulu*, he has written the libretti for *Whitsunday* and *Love Burns*. Telemovies are *Displaced Persons, Hunger* and *The Lizard King*. He wrote the screenplays for *Map of the Human Heart, Cosi, Heaven's Burning* and *Radiance*. He lives in Sydney.

ABOUT LOUIS NOWRA

The Theatre of Louis Nowra by Veronica Kelly

Louis Nowra's work is highly theatrical, blackly comic and draws on references from Ovid and Shakespeare to horror movies and tabloid newspapers. In her compelling study, Veronica Kelly draws out the sources of Nowra's passionate, idiosyncratic vision and demonstrates how it reveals the turbulance at the root of Australian history.

Veronica Kelly is Associate Professor in Drama in the English Department of Queensland University. The book includes a full list of Nowra's works and a select bibliography.

THE GOLDEN AGE

Louis Nowra

Introduction by
Gerry Turcotte

Currency Press • Sydney

First published in 1985 by
Currency Press,
PO Box 2287,
Strawberry Hills NSW 2012
enquiries@currency.com.au; www.currency.com.au

Reprinted 1988.

This revised edition first published 1989

Reprinted 1992, 1995, 1998, 2000, 2004

NATIONAL LIBRARY OF AUSTRALIA CATALOGUING-IN-PUBLICATION DATA:
Nowra, Louis, 1950–
    The golden age
    2nd ed.
    ISBN 0 86819 234 1
    I. Title
    A822.3

Typeset by Renwick Pride Pty Ltd, Albury, NSW
Printed by McPherson's Printing Group, Maryborough
Cover design by Hana Rocak

This publication has been assisted by the Commonwealth
Government through the Australia Council, its arts funding
and advisory body.

There are moments when speech is but a mouth pressed lightly and humbly against the angel's hand.

James Merrill

In memory of Marvin Gaye.

Above: Dennis Clements as Peter, Richard Roxburgh as Francis, Bruce Hughes as Mac, Jeanette Cronin as Ayre, Stuart Halcroft as Melorne, Rosemary Haris as Betsheb, Mark McAskill as Stef, Victoria Eagger as Angel. Below: Melinda Marcellos as Dr Simon, Keith Agius as William Archer, Rosemary Haris as Betsheb, Mark McAskill as Stef. NIDA production. Photos: Peter Holderness.

Keith Agius as William Archer, Rosemary Haris as Betsheb, Mark McAskill as Stef. NIDA production. Photo: Peter Holderness.

Above: Melita Jurisic as Betsheb and Terry O'Brien as Stef. Playbox production. Photo: D.B. Simmonds/Sterio Stills. Below: Rosemary Haris as Betsheb and Richard Roxburgh as Francis. NIDA production. Photo: Peter Holderness.

Contents

Preface

Louis Nowra

The origins of *The Golden Age* probably lie in my final year of high school. We had a small library run by a very large, grey-haired woman who showed an extraordinary interest (for the late 1960s) in Australian literature. One day she told me that she was reading a novel set in Tasmania. Although the book wasn't very good, it contained the memorable line, 'She was a wild thing amidst classical furniture.' The line has stayed with me ever since and I think its resonance echoes loudly throughout the play.

The origins of the story itself lie with an academic whom I met at Monash university in 1984. He told me the story of how two men had come across a strange group of people in the wilds of South-West Tasmania just before World War II. The story he told me is basically the play, including the fact that the men took the group back to Hobart but because they seemed to confirm Nazi theories of genetic and racial degeneration, the group was placed in New Norfolk Asylum. In his story the group died before the war ended. He thought that the story about the group might be factual and that a friend, an historian, was trying to find out if there was, indeed, any truth to it. I don't know what he discovered, nor did I care. Entranced by the story I started to write the play.

Coincidentally, while I was writing the play, I found myself in Tasmania where I visited the ruins of the prison settlement, Port Arthur. It was there that my thoughts about the play truly crystallised. I had never seen a whole town devoted to the mental and physical destruction of human beings. The truly terrible thing was how such

human barbarism could exist amidst such natural
beauty. Walking through the ruins I could almost hear
the cries of the victims of what Ayre calls 'rack 'n' cat'.
My next step was to invent the language. I read books
about lower class language and slang in the 1840s and
books of the bawdy verse of the times. I thought that this
group, isolated from the outside world for three
generations, would have turned upside-down society's
notions of obscene language and used it as a non-vulgar
vehicle to explain notions of fertility and the like.
Listening to the several productions I have seen, I think
that the language becomes clearer when spoken with a
kind of Irish rhythm. It also becomes obvious that the
language should be spoken as clearly as possible, so that
by the end of the play the audience understands most of
it.

Another crucial aspect for a production is to get the
anthropology of the group right. The group (or, as some
people call them, 'the tribe') should have, in the minds of
the actors and director, a true reality; they are not fairy
people. Like the Aborigines who were once common in
Tasmania, the tribe should have its own customs, true
communications with language and the dynamics of
interpersonal relationships.

This version of the play is the complete one and differs
in many ways from Currency's Current Theatre Series
edition. One of the most obvious differences from the
earlier edition is that I have added a new scene in Act
One. This scene was in my original script but was left out
of the premiere production for several reasons. I feel
that the scene is crucial in that it describes the world of
the Archers, sketches in a little better the relationship
between Peter and Francis and supplies the *Alice in
Wonderland* metaphor. Like Alice, Francis falls down a
hole into another world.

It must be pointed out that *The Golden Age* is no
polemic about civilisation and nature. The play is not
saying that nature is good and civilisation evil. It is also
not saying that the group is innocent and wonderful and

the civilised people are evil. Both groups have their good and bad aspects and the relationship between the two is more subtle than that. While I'm on this point of interpretation, I should also say that the ending (one of my most optimistic) is not a hippie pastoral — far from it. Francis has taken Betsheb back to her home. What he is going to do next will be a major problem, as Peter very well knows. The important thing for Francis, however, is that, for the moment, he has saved her. I suppose, then, that one could call *The Golden Age* a love story. Betsheb and Francis make a strange duo; nevertheless, if they have anything in common, it is that they are outsiders.

Sydenham
July, 1988

Introduction

Gerry Turcotte

In 1939, a lost tribe of white Europeans was apparently discovered in the Tasmanian wilderness. These nineteenth-century emigres suffered from serious genetic malformations, and the Australian government, fearing their condition could be used by Nazi propagandists, secreted the tribe in an asylum pending the end of the war. They did not survive the internment; all died of tuberculosis.

This grim tragedy is the basis for what is surely Louis Nowra's most accomplished play, a work which blends poetic language, historical fact, Australian folklore and Greek mythology. For *The Golden Age* is about history and empires; it is about humanity's responsibility to itself; and it is about the importance of language, art and tradition to that humanist vision. It is an ambitious work which does not betray its objectives.

The Golden Age is set principally in Tasmania, though it does move briefly to war-torn Berlin. It divides most of its time between Hobart and a wilderness described as 'one of the most unexplored regions on earth', as an 'underworld' and as 'the burial ground to nature'; a place so remote as to have allowed a group of people — a colony in miniature — to survive unmolested by the twentieth century. It is in this latter landscape that two young bushwalkers first discover the lost tribe, and it is their presence, evocative of a wider world, which convinces the matriarch of the colony to abandon the wilderness of exile and rejoin civilisation.

The conceit of the two worlds is a useful paradigm for Nowra's questioning of such values as are attached to the primitive, the civilised, the legitimate and the illegitimate. For despite the colony's archaic rituals, its genetic malformations, its infertility and imminent demise, Nowra can effectively contrast its world with the chaos of a civilisation which, despite its supposedly greater knowledge and sophistication, is nevertheless about to engage in a world war. The parallel begs the question: how can the modern world consider itself superior to supposedly simpler societies, when it cannot even save itself from the most simplistic of solutions to political complexities: war?

The play-within-a-play allows Nowra to demonstrate the tenuous position of great empires which are traditionally held up as examples of the power and merit of high culture. The Greek theatrical fragments show not only the pettiness and cruelty at the heart of these worlds, but also suggest that even they will crumble and degenerate. The force of time, or the darkness of the human soul, and not any inherent genetic weakness, is at the heart of humanity's inexorable decline. *Iphigenia in Tauris*, set in the crumbling Greek temple of a Tasmanian garden, prefigures the major themes of *The Golden Age* and comments obliquely yet relevantly on its meaning.

Of course, *The Golden Age* is not merely concerned with universals. It is also a frank study of the Australian landscape — its people and its history. The Tasmanian wilderness stands, in part, as a metaphor for the Australian unconscious, a representation of its dreams and hopes — the quest for freedom and fortune — but also of its darkest fears — the threat of isolation and imminent decay. The lost tribe, headed by the indomitable Queenie Ayre, stands as an uncomfortable reminder of the all the 'good' untapped by, and all the possible tragedies available to, humanity. Because the colonists so unequivocally embody best and worst, however, they are difficult for society to bear; they are an embarrassment to be locked away in an asylum and forgotten.

But *The Golden Age* is not about forgetting. As always in Louis Nowra's work, the play's focus is on forcing a society to come to terms with its errors, and to explore those factors which have made mistakes possible. One of the primary errors with which Nowra is concerned is white Australia's treatment of Aboriginal peoples. His hugely successful adaptation for the stage of Xavier Herbert's epic novel *Capricornia* focused critical attention on his commitment to the issue of race relations between Aborigines and white Australians. If many critics were surprised at Nowra's skill in delineating this conflict, it could only have been because they had failed to read his previous work more closely.

Levels of oppression and inequality generally, and the conflict between Aborigines and white Australians specifically, have always been chief concerns of Nowra's work. In early plays he made the former preoccupation quite clear. *Albert Names Edward*, *Inner Voices*, and *Visions* all focus on powerful figures in control of facts, language and information; figures, moreover, who use this power to further their own ambitions. Albert manipulates the amnesic Edward to guarantee a measure of immortality for himself; Ivan is similarly controlled by the court followers to escape drudgery and gain political security; and Madame Lynch and her husband, in the last of the abovementioned plays, sacrifice their country and its traditions for the visions of other nations and for the lifestyles and beliefs of other peoples.

Inside the Island sharpens the focus of Nowra's concerns with indigenous peoples (already obvious in *Visions*), and brings his investigations closer to home. He eschews the foreign landscape for Australian soil, and international metaphors of imperialism and oppression for more local examples. With *Sunrise* he again demonstrates that the act of privileging one race over another — one way of seeing and interpreting the world — is fruitless and, ultimately, destructive. The 'visions' of Clarrie and Venice, representing as they do European and indigenous points of view respectively, suggest

strongly that only through unity of perspective can races
hope to survive; alone they can only perish. More
critically, he shows that white perspectives do not allow
for the native vision to survive; they ruthlessly eliminate,
or they try through coercive influence to eradicate, that
vision.

It is in *The Golden Age*, however, that Louis Nowra
makes this focus most powerfully felt. Reading on a
number of different levels and according to a number of
different influences, many critics have curiously failed to
see that the play's strongest comments are directed at
race relations and that it makes an impassioned plea not
for racial tolerance but for racial harmony and
understanding. In two specific areas, the more
pessimistic and short-sighted of Nowra's characters draw
the parallel between the lost tribe and Aborigines
directly, one going so far as to say: 'They were like those
Aboriginal tribes that withered away because their
culture wasn't strong enough. It happens in nature, in
human civilisations, one big animal swallows a little one.'
But far from endorsing this shallow Darwinism, Nowra
attacks the notion by offering the madness of war as the
stronger civilisation's only legacy. Materialism and the
blind pursuit of power are shown to be destructive, and
history concurs. The memory of the Greek tragedy still
echoes in the mind: Elizabeth Archer's magnificent
culture has decayed. Iphigenia and Orestes, as hindsight
suggests, return to a crumbling empire.

The notion of the decline of great traditions and
lineages is central to the drama. A very effective parallel
is made, for example, between the degeneracy of the clan
and that of the stronger culture which sneers at what it
deems to be primitive. In one scene, a government
official expresses his surprise that so few generations
were needed to give birth to the autistic Stef. And yet, as
Nowra shows in a later passage, it takes 'enlightened'
contemporary society even less time to destroy the family
of outcasts and to reduce Francis to the level of a
murderer. As Francis himself puts it:

How could I describe what I was seeing? Civilisations perfecting death. Bombs, fighter planes, slaughtered soldiers, extermination camps, rape, blood lust ... I couldn't write any more gentle letters because I have nothing of that left inside me any more ... I knew I couldn't go home again. This prison perfectly suits my state of mind; I have been bred for it, just as I have been bred to kill ... It's as if this century has imagined a monster, concocted it from the deepest underworld of its brain and now it has escaped and is devouring everything. Nothing makes sense.

Typically, Peter retorts, 'Your bitterness will pass.'

Not surprisingly, Francis becomes, and Betsheb continues to be, an outcast. All of Nowra's plays, in fact, are preoccupied with the outcasts of society. And usually he explores their dilemma through their difficulties with language — their inability to find a suitable voice with which to speak. The main characters are either inarticulate, as with Edward and Ivan, or they speak an unusable or inappropriate language, as with Juana and Venice (in *Albert Names Edward, Inner Voices, Visions and Sunrise* respectively). In *The Golden Age* this focus remains; one could even say it finds its most powerful metaphor in the colourful 'word salad' which the outcasts speak. Made up of Irish rhythms, English bawdy verse and early convict slang, the language reflects both the vitality and ritualistic strength of the colony, as well as its hereditary weaknesses. (Many of their pronunciations, for example, are the result of speaking with a cleft palate, or of being taught the language by a person who had one.) In this way, the language, like so much in this rich play stands as a metaphor for the tribe's position between worlds, and of its attempts to create a new language which will more adequately represent the new world. In the course of discovering such a language, Nowra's protagonists create new countries to inhabit, both of the mind and body.

Essentially all of Nowra's plays, as he himself has put it, deal with the problem of 'whose view of the world will prevail'. This is especially true of *The Golden Age* which most successfully represents the concretisation of his bleak — though not defeatist — view of humankind. It is a powerful vision of a world perched on the lip of destruction; a world which has lost its way. If there is a message in his plays, it is that humanity must examine the past for its errors — not to duplicate, but to learn from them. His is a message of reconciliation with the children of the land, a spiritual 're-visioning' that will be hard to enact, but which must be done. *The Golden Age* not only voices this plea, it offers its most articulate phrasing. 'Nowt more outcastin'', a cry heard throughout the play, is an appeal for all to listen.

The University of Sydney
March, 1989

THE GOLDEN AGE

The Golden Age was first performed by the Playbox Theatre Company at the Studio Theatre of the Victorian Arts Centre on 8 February 1985 with the following cast:

WILLIAM/MELORNE	Robin Cuming
ELIZABETH/ANGEL/ DR SIMON	Marilynne Hanigan
STEF/PRIVATE CORRIS	Terry O'Brien
AYRE/MRS WITCOMBE	Maggie Blinco
MAC/GEORGE ROSS/JAMES/ GERMAN MAN	Mark Minchinton
PETER	Andrew Sharp
FRANCIS	Robert Morgan
BETSHEB	Melita Jurisic

Directed by Rex Cramphorn
Designed by Shaun Gurton
Lighting Design by John Beckett
Original Music by Sarah de Jong

Cover photographs: Back: Melita Jurisic as Betsheb, Maggie Blinco as Ayre, Robin Cuming as Melorne. Front: Melita Jurisic. Playbox production.
Photos: D.B. Simmonds/Sterio Stills.

CHARACTERS

WILLIAM ARCHER, a doctor
ELIZABETH ARCHER, WILLIAM's wife
FRANCIS MORRIS, a young engineer
PETER ARCHER, a young geologist
BETSHEB, a young woman
STEF, an 'autistic' child
AYRE, an old woman
MELORNE, an old man
ANGEL, a woman in her twenties
MAC, a young man
GEORGE ROSS, M.P., Federal Minister for Health
MRS WITCOMBE, a working class woman in her fifties
DR SIMON, psychiatrist at the asylum
JAMES, a patient at the asylum
PRIVATE CORRIS, an Australian soldier
A GERMAN MAN, a man on the run
MARY, a maid
A servant

SETTING

The play is set during the wartime years 1939-45, and the action moves from locations in Hobart and South-West Tasmania to Berlin in the last days of the War.

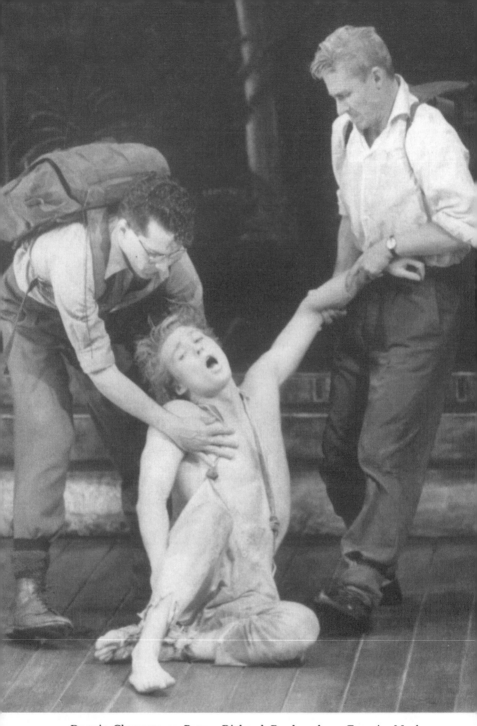

Dennis Clements as Peter, Richard Roxburgh as Francis, Mark
McAskill as Stef. NIDA production. Photo: Peter Holderness.

ACT ONE

SCENE ONE

Hobart, 1939. A garden. It is a hot Australian night full of the sounds of cicadas and crickets. ELIZABETH ARCHER, *a middle-aged woman, stands in front of a small, crumbling Greek temple. She wears a copy of an ancient Greek dress. For a moment it seems we are in ancient Greece, but she is playing* Iphigenia *from* Iphigenia in Tauris.

ELIZABETH: 'I dreamed I had escaped from this island and lived at home in Argos. There I was asleep when suddenly the earth shook and tore apart. I ran outdoors and helplessly watched the whole house crumble into the earth. Out of this ruin, which was my father's house, one column stood. Brown hair grew from its head and it spoke in a human voice. Weeping, I performed for it this murderous ritual for strangers, sprinkling water, as on one destined to die. I interpret this dream thus: it was my brother Orestes I prepared for death and he has died. For what are pillars of a house but its sons. And those whose heads I touch with purifying water die. So now I want to pour libations for my brother.'

[WILLIAM, *about the same age as his wife, enters as Orestes. He is handcuffed, wears glasses and a dinner jacket. He stands before Iphigenia.*]

'Do you know where you are?'

WILLIAM: 'Tauris, my High Priestess.'

ELIZABETH: 'And what is it known for?'

WILLIAM: 'Any Greek who lands on its shores is put to death.'

ELIZABETH: 'And yet, mysterious stranger, you are Greek and you dare to step on our island. You should have left when you had the chance.'

WILLIAM: 'I was shipwrecked.'

ELIZABETH: 'I do not believe your story. Do you see the

dark stain on the altar? It is the blood of previous
sacrifices. Your blood will mingle with that blood to
delight the goddess Artemis.'

WILLIAM: 'I would not care to die if my sister were here
to prepare me for my burial.'

ELIZABETH: 'A hopeless wish for a lost soul. Your sister
would never be in this savage country. I gather you
were captured with another man.'

WILLIAM: 'My friend Pylades. He is rich, his house is pure
and untainted while I live nowhere and everywhere. I
am an outcast, hated by the gods.'

ELIZABETH: 'I too am far from home and live only to
perform these dark rites which are so savage as not to
be sung. Last night I dreamed my brother, whom I
have not seen since we were children, was dead. Killed.
His house in ruins. I now have nothing left to lose.
Cruelty has overtaken me, possessed me. You are the
first to sail here in a long time but you will never return
home. You will die in pain and lie in an unmarked
grave.'

SCENE TWO

*The same place, next morning. A servant sets up outdoor tables
and chairs. Off, in the distance,* FRANCIS *and* PETER *play
tennis. While the servant sets up,* MR TURNER *enters. He is
blind and confused. The servant doesn't see him and heads off,
humming, to get another chair.* MR TURNER *hears.*

MR TURNER: Am I in the garden?
    [*The servant doesn't respond.*]
  Excuse me, am I in the garden?
    [*Silence. He goes a little further and finds himself on the
    steps of the temple. This confuses him further.*]
  Hello, is anybody here?
    [*He enters the temple and disappears.*]

[*Off*] Mrs Archer?
[*The servant re-enters with another chair, followed by* WILLIAM.]
WILLIAM: I admire the boy's stamina playing in this heat.
ELIZABETH: [*entering behind him*] His driver said he dropped him at the front door and now he's disappeared. Vanished!
[*She exits again. The boys appear.* PETER *looks very English in his whites.* FRANCIS *wears tennis shoes with football socks, a T-shirt and black football shorts.*]
WILLIAM: Who won?
PETER: Francis, by a whisker.
FRANCIS: By a mile.
[*They laugh.* PETER *pours lemonade for his friend and himself.*]
WILLIAM: [*to* FRANCIS] You know what you two are about to do is quite dangerous.
PETER: Don't nag, father.
WILLIAM: Francis, didn't Mary lay out some tennis whites for you?
[FRANCIS *is embarrassed.*]
PETER: She did, but Francis didn't know they were for him.
[ELIZABETH *enters.*]
ELIZABETH: I can't find him anywhere.
WILLIAM: He'll turn up.
ELIZABETH: I want to personally give him his cheque. I think the School for the Blind should be quite pleased at how much was given last night. [*Glancing at* FRANCIS' *clothes*] Francis, didn't Mary — ?
WILLIAM: [*interrupting*] We've been through that.
ELIZABETH: [*sitting*] The weather is exquisite! Have you been to Tasmania before, Francis?
FRANCIS: First time. Thank you for letting me stay here —
ELIZABETH: [*waving this away*] Our pleasure. Half the time we think we're a separate country from the rest of Australia.
[*The boys finish their lemonade.*]

PETER: We'll go and clean up.

ELIZABETH: Make it snappy. I'd like you to meet Mr Turner.

[*The boys exit.*]

Did you speak to them about their trip?

WILLIAM: They're determined.

ELIZABETH: They should consider something less hazardous.

WILLIAM: It's part of the attraction.

[MR TURNER *emerges from the temple behind them, lost and confused.*]

ELIZABETH: That Francis, he's a strange boy. I watched him playing tennis from the balcony. He plays with such ferocity.

WILLIAM: It's why I like him, he's had to fight so hard to get where he is.

MR TURNER: Hello?

[ELIZABETH *turns around.*]

ELIZABETH: Mr Turner! [*Rushing to his aid*] Stay where you are.

MR TURNER: Where am I?

ELIZABETH: On the steps of the temple.

MR TURNER: Temple?

[ELIZABETH *grabs him and escorts him to the chairs.*]

ELIZABETH: I've been looking everywhere for you.

MR TURNER: [*still confused*] I thought I was in the garden, and then ...

ELIZABETH: Sit down ... Some lemonade? [*Pouring it without waiting for an answer*] You seem flustered.

WILLIAM: How are you, Mr Turner?

MR TURNER: Is that you, Mr Archer?

WILLIAM: Yes.

ELIZABETH: [*putting the glass in his hand*] There you are. You certainly won't be going home empty handed, Mr Turner. The Greek tragedy wrought a financial miracle.

MR TURNER: I was lost.

ELIZABETH: Excuse me?

MR TURNER: I thought I was in the garden. I smelt roses.

Flowers. And then I stepped into another world. I felt
like Alice in Wonderland. I said 'Hello' and it echoed
all about me. I was lost. I thought I was dead.
[*The Archers have no idea what he is talking about.*]

SCENE THREE

---

*The wilds of south-west Tasmania, evening. Two lanterns sit
on the ground.* FRANCIS, *tired and dirty, rests against his
knapsack looking at a map in the frail light cast by the lantern.
He eats some biscuits.*

FRANCIS: [*to himself*] Jesus ...
    [*Silence.*]
    [*Calling*] Are you all right?
    [*No answer.*]
    Peter?
PETER: [*off*] Coming!
    [FRANCIS *returns to his map.*]
FRANCIS: Could be anywhere ... anywhere.
    [*A noise comes from the bush behind him.* FRANCIS
    looks.]
    Peter?
    [*Silence.*]
    Is that you, Peter?
    [*Silence. There is nothing.* FRANCIS *returns to his map.*
    PETER *enters from another direction, exhausted and
    dirty.*]
PETER: Got bloody caught up in the Bauera.
FRANCIS: The what?
PETER: That wild rose we saw this morning. It grows
around everything and once it's entangled all living
things, it grows back on itself to form a wall. A bit like
my mother.
    [*He sits down and takes a stone from his pocket.*]
I found this: it was glinting in the moonlight. [*Taking
a closer look at it under the lantern*] I'll have a better look

at it in the morning. Once you conquered this region I'm sure you'd find huge mineral deposits.

FRANCIS: I'd be happy if we could conquer this map. We should go back the way we came, otherwise we'll get well and truly lost. Not that we're not anyway.

PETER: [unconcerned] We'll be fine. Do you know that this part of Tasmania is one of the most unexplored regions on earth, like the Amazon or the highlands of New Guinea? [Standing] It's like another world, isn't it?

FRANCIS: [looking up at the night sky] Can't even see the stars.

PETER: An underworld. [Jumping up and down] See how the ground springs?

FRANCIS: Soggy.

PETER: You know we're about ten foot off the ground?
    [FRANCIS laughs.]
True. We're on the burial ground of nature. Rotten vegetable residue of centuries, ancient and petrified trees. So here we are, suspended ten foot above the true floor.

FRANCIS: That's what I love about nature; it's so treacherous.

PETER: You look at nature and your eyes glaze over.

FRANCIS: I always feel that I'm looking at a postcard. [Smiling] My mother says that nature is God's Bible.

PETER: You know, you've never introduced me to her.

FRANCIS: Things that humans make: cars, gas works, factories: now that's something. The conquering of chaos.

PETER: You're serious?

FRANCIS: A painter does a painting and people think it's a miracle. It is more wonderful to see a blueprint of a building or bridge and watch it transformed into reality. The Sydney Harbour Bridge has not only conquered nature but is also beautiful. It is imagination made concrete. Mind has become matter.
    [PETER laughs.]
What are you laughing at?

PETER: [*slightly bewildered*] Nothing.

FRANCIS: Take your father; he's an artist, he heals the sick. That's more important than painting. He saves lives.

[FRANCIS *notices something.*]

PETER: In a way.

FRANCIS: Did you see that?

PETER: Probably some animal.

[PETER *goes through his knapsack.*]

FRANCIS: I heard something over there before.

PETER: Sorry to put you through the ordeal of meeting my parents.

FRANCIS: It was interesting.

[PETER *laughs.*]

PETER: They have developed certain eccentricities.

FRANCIS: I heard you arguing with your dad before we left.

PETER: He doesn't want me to go to Europe; he thinks the political climate is 'unsuitable'. Since he became president of the Medical Board he's taken an unnatural interest in politics. Like you. At the moment he's trying to get the medical profession to protest against the deregistration of Jewish doctors in Germany. I say to him, 'Why bother? Australians don't give a damn.'

FRANCIS: [*sarcastically*] Perhaps the English will.

PETER: Who cares, anyway? I want to enjoy myself over there; get to know my mother's relatives, Esther's family —

FRANCIS: [*interrupting*] Esther's family?

PETER: She's partly why I'm going.

FRANCIS: You're not marrying her?

PETER: When I return.

FRANCIS: I thought you said you wanted to enjoy life. Think of all the women you'll never get to know.

PETER: You boys from the slums.

FRANCIS: I have my standards: I only go out with rich girls; I'm trying to rise above my class.

PETER: Is that why you mix with me?

FRANCIS: Of course. You're my introductory service.

> [*Suddenly a woman screams. Both men jump up. The scream goes on and on, anguished, passionate but almost ritualistic.*]

PETER: What in the hell is that?

> [*It goes on, then abruptly stops. Silence. Both boys are scared.*]

That was a person, wasn't it?

FRANCIS: No animal could sound like that.

PETER: Maybe it was an animal in pain.

> [*They take their lanterns and go to the area from which they judge the cry came.*]

FRANCIS: Here.

> [PETER *comes over and shines his lantern. It reveals the corpse of a young man, his body covered in rotten flowers.*]

PETER: Christ, I'm going to be sick.

> [*He moves away.* FRANCIS *holds his lantern closer and examines the body.*]

FRANCIS: He's been dead for some time. I wonder why no one's buried him. They've covered him in flowers; why not bury him, then?

PETER: Perhaps someone wanted him left that way.

FRANCIS: He seems quite young.

PETER: God, he stinks. How can you be so close?

FRANCIS: There's something about his face ...

PETER: It's rotten, that's all. Come on, Francis, let's get going. That screaming ...

FRANCIS: It'll take us days to get back.

> [FRANCIS *spots something.*]

Jesus ...

> [*He holds the lantern closer.*]

PETER: What is it?

FRANCIS: His mouth is full of gold.

> [PETER *comes closer.* FRANCIS *takes out a small piece.*]

See?

PETER: You're like my father: nothing bothers you.

FRANCIS: [*handing the gold piece to* PETER] See?

PETER: [*repulsed*] No thanks, not from a dead man's mouth.
[*Silence. Unnoticed, the silhouetted figure of a woman enters.*]
FRANCIS: Flowers ... bits of gold ...
PETER: Perhaps he was murdered.
FRANCIS: Why would a murderer do this to him? Anyway, you told me nobody is supposed to be living way out here.
[*The woman growls softly at* FRANCIS *and* PETER. *Both boys are startled. They stand up and look at her.* BETSHEB *is young, dirty, and dressed in a nineteenth-century dress patched in various colours as if repaired over many years. She bares her teeth at them, almost like an animal, then screams violently as if cursing them. She turns and runs away. Blackout.*]

SCENE FOUR

A river bank, afternoon. BETSHEB *sits on the bank with* STEF, *a boy aged between fifteen and eighteen. It is hard to tell his exact age because his behaviour is so infantile. His limbs seem spastic. His gaze is distant. The woman wears the same dress as before. The boy wears only a filthy pair of long johns, years old. The woman chews up a piece of meat and passes it into the boy's mouth by placing her mouth on his, like a bird feeding its chick. He is not very hungry and protests. She gets up and goes to the river where she wets a rag. As she does so she hums to herself a tune reminiscent of a Victorian ballad. While she wets the rag the boy tries to stand, but flops down and in the process tumbles over. The woman sees him and laughs. The boy finds himself flat on his back, like a beetle that cannot right itself, as his legs and arms don't function properly. Even though he wants to get up he doesn't call out. Eventually he rights himself. The woman comes over as the boy begins to crawl towards something of interest, like a crippled child in a Muybridge photograph. The effort is too great and he flops down. The woman wipes his face, then her own. She then blows loudly and theatrically on his face, pretending to be the wind. The boy pathetically tries to mimic her. She stands up and spins around in her beloved dress for him. He takes no notice, his eyes looking past her. Abruptly she drops to her knees and slaps him on the face. He yelps in pain. She kisses him where she has hit him and then moves away so he can see her properly. She smiles broadly and stiffly, trying to teach him. She pushes at his mouth until it turns into a smile, but when she lets go his face returns to its expressionless mask. She is frustrated. She hums. He follows suit, but his gaze is distant. She bites his leg and he yelps in pain. As he cries out she mimics him. He looks at her for a brief moment, then beyond her. The routine is over. The woman gets up and does a whirling dervish-like dance and hums loudly to herself. Suddenly she notices something and stops. Frightened, she runs to the boy and tries to drag him off, but he is angry and fights. She drops him and heads off. She exits and moments later* FRANCIS *hurries on, followed by* PETER.

FRANCIS: [*calling after her*] Hey!
    [*He runs after her.* PETER *walks over to* STEF.]
PETER: Hello!
    [*The boy doesn't seem to notice him.* FRANCIS *returns.*]
FRANCIS: My God, she's quick. Lost her.
    [PETER *waves his hand in front of the boy's face.*]
  Is he blind?
PETER: Maybe.
    [*Suddenly the boy's hand snakes out and grabs* PETER'*s hand.* PETER *is startled. The boy laughs, then bites the hand.* PETER *cries out in pain.*]
FRANCIS: What happened?
PETER: He bit it.
    [*Silence.*]
FRANCIS: [*to the boy*] What's your name?
    [*Pause.*]
  Your name, what is it?
    [*The boy rolls over, not listening, and laughs at the sky.*]
PETER: What's he laughing at?
    [*Suddenly the boy's mood changes. He grimaces.*]

[*To the boy*] Are you all right?

[*The boy groans loudly, rising to a sharply accentuated crescendo until, abruptly, he bursts into a wide grin. Then he moves on all fours, but the effort is too much and he collapses. His face goes blank and his eyes distant.* FRANCIS *and* PETER *don't know what to make of it all.*]

PETER: [*laughing nervously*] I wouldn't mind not being here.

FRANCIS: We'd better pull him back or he might fall into the river.

[*They grab hold of the boy and drag him back from the river. The boy takes no notice of what is happening to him.* BETSHEB *silently enters and stands nervously nearby.* PETER *is the first to notice her.*]

PETER: [*quietly*] Francis.

[FRANCIS *turns and spots her. She is now extremely nervous. She sinks to her knees and dry-retches with fear. The two young men don't know what to do. The woman crawls on all fours to the boy and makes sure he is all right. She slaps him hard. He laughs. She laboriously lifts him on her back.* FRANCIS *goes to help, but* PETER *holds him back.*]

She knows how to do it.

[*The boy clings to her back like a monkey. The woman goes off without looking at the two intruders. Silence.*]

FRANCIS: Come on.

PETER: What?

FRANCIS: Scared?

PETER: Pain in the arse.

[*They exit after her.*]

SCENE FIVE

A clearing, afternoon. Four people wait: AYRE, *an old woman, sits on a homemade wooden chair; the others sit on the ground.* ANGEL *is in her late twenties. She is pale and coughs occasionally.* MELORNE, *a strong and wiry old white-haired man sits near her.* MAC, *a twenty-year-old man with blond hair sits by himself. They are dressed in old odds and ends, as though they have been to a Victorian opportunity shop. They seem expectant and their pose is like that of a Victorian photograph. On the ground are some wooden and chipped-porcelain bowls. Some pieces of meat lie near the bowls; there are also seeds, wild fruit and flowers. There is a large wash bowl in the centre of this arrangement. They wait some time and then* BETSHEB *enters, half dragging, half carrying* STEF. *He grins widely as if at some private joke. She drops him down near the others. Just then* FRANCIS *and* PETER *enter. They are startled at the scene before them. All except the boy and old woman rise and bow deeply but stiffly towards the boys. Silence.*

FRANCIS: [*pointing*] We followed that girl.
    [*Silence. Everyone is nervous and apprehensive. As the old woman speaks the words make little sense to the boys.*]
AYRE: To the greeny pallor o' thee kingspot; o' cunty goldy.
    [PETER *smiles, amused.* FRANCIS *realises it is a welcome.*]
FRANCIS: Thank you. My name is Francis. This is Peter. We come from Hobart.
    [*Silence. They don't seem to understand.*]
    [*Pointing to himself*] Francis. [*To* PETER] Peter.
    [*The old lady nods and motions to the young woman, who goes to her.*]
AYRE: Betsheb. [*Pointing to the old man*] Melorne. [*To the woman*] Angel. [*To the autistic boy*] Stef. [*To the young man*] Mac. [*To herself*] Ayre.
PETER: Hello.
FRANCIS: Hello.
    [*The pair are amused by the situation.* AYRE *motions to the others to find their places. There is something of an unconscious parody about the group, as if with their limited means they are giving an upper-class tea party.*]
PETER: [*to* FRANCIS] I think we're invited to a tea party.
FRANCIS: Did you understand her?

PETER: [*amused*] Not a word.

[AYRE *stays in her chair.*]

AYRE: [*smiling*] I bunter t' the windy sheet, t' the arsemine o' the world. Breathe a vein, breathe a vein. [*Shaking her head*] Olcers an' 'ellpain. [*Tapping her chair*] Starry, shiny, cunty dell o' me world.

[*It is obvious she is trying to explain why she can't join the others. The visitors sit.* AYRE *claps her hands and motions to* ANGEL, *who picks up an old-fashioned porcelain doll and shows it to* FRANCIS.]

FRANCIS: It's lovely. Very old.

[ANGEL *smiles and nods.* MELORNE *walks into the centre of the group, picks up a washbowl and shows it to the two men proudly.*]

PETER: [*looking into the bowl*] Gold. It must have taken a long time to collect all those tiny pieces.

[MELORNE *puts the bowl back in its position.*]

FRANCIS: [*to* MELORNE] We saw a dead man on the mountain. Back there. He had flowers in his hair and gold in his mouth.

[MELORNE *sits, uncomprehending.* FRANCIS *points to* BETSHEB.]

She came and cried beside him.

[STEF *lies on his back and makes wind noises at the sky.*]

PETER: He wasn't buried, but he was dead.

[*No one seems to understand.* BETSHEB *hands meat and fruit to* FRANCIS *and* PETER *in the only two porcelain bowls.*]

PETER: [*to* FRANCIS, *sotto voce*] I see we get the best china. [*To* BETSHEB] Thank you.

FRANCIS: How long have you people lived here?

[*Silence.*]

Do you understand us?

[*Silence.*]

MELORNE: [*thickly*] Fer skilly we gobble in awe.

[BETSHEB *and* AYRE *both laugh, as at a private joke. Everyone starts to eat. They have spoons and / or battered forks. There is an embarrassing silence as people try and think of ways of bridging the gap.*]

FRANCIS: [*at last*] I come from Melbourne. Peter comes from Hobart. I'm an engineer. I design bridges. Peter is a geologist. He studies rocks. He knows all about things like that gold there.
> [*No one seems to understand.* BETSHEB *feeds* STEF *by the same method she used before.* AYRE *sees the visitors' surprise.*]

AYRE: Born o' cat 'n' rack 'n' goldy sow.
> [*They don't understand. Annoyed at being fed when he doesn't want to be,* STEF *cries out and rolls away.* ANGEL *begins to hum a tune.*]

He fed on tarse o' dark in the black quim o' a belle.
> [STEF *joins* ANGEL *in humming the snatch of melody, but soon he grows very loud.*]
> [*Trying to make herself understood*] Skittle. Skittle. Blackfortune.
> [*The two men nod as though they can understand.* STEF's *humming is almost yelling now.* PETER *recognises the tune and begins to sing over the top of* STEF; *he goes beyond the snatch of tune and sings the whole verse.*]

PETER:

> 'I finally found you', Edward said.
> 'I've just returned from the salt, salt sea,
> And it is all for the love of thee.
> They say you married a hanging judge,
> O don't let the news, the news be true.
> But a friend, he said you didn't wait for me
> As I have waited on the sea for you.'

> [*There is a silence, except for the quiet humming of* STEF. PETER *is embarrassed.*]

Those are the words of that song. My grandmother taught them to me.
> [ANGEL *gives an 1850s top hat in very good condition to* MELORNE. *He makes a performing space.* BETSHEB *drags* STEF *to lie at* AYRE's *feet.* STEF *stops humming and briefly cries out in alarm.* AYRE *pats him on the head and sings a murmuring song.*]

AYRE: [*singing*]

> In the night,
> In the day,
> Blue ruins, blue ruins
> In Jack's Inn Bay.

[*The two young men become the audience for the others. The four bow to them. As they perform, the words sometimes seem out of keeping with their emotions, as if they, especially* MELORNE, *don't always understand what they are saying.*]

MELORNE: Bleak street o' fen 'n' bellies. Dark trees 'n' no trees betide bleak sand.

[*The scene set, he begins. He grabs* MAC *and drags him as if through terrible country. He stops.*]

[*Yelling, to* MAC] 'Toady o' the holy! Bleak King o' the dark. Thou walk on loam cooked o' thou disease. Thou disease pox on the land in blood 'n' pig. [*Indicating the land and sky*] 'Rye o' the sky, rye o' the loam. Morn 'n' dark all topsy turvy.' [*Motioning to himself*] 'I, King. King o' cits.' [*Crying out*] 'Trellion! Trellion!'

[MAC *sings to entertain the tormented* MELORNE. ANGEL *plays a penny whistle to accompany him. She plays well.*]

MAC: [*singing*]

> Up 'n' down
> He go,
> Up 'n' down
> A-jig, jig, jig.
> She go
> Groan 'n' groan
> A-jig, jig, jig.

[MELORNE *pats* MAC *on the head as one would a favourite dog.*]

MELORNE: 'A-lik a-lik a-lik a-lik a-lik ...'

[ANGEL *enters and throws herself at* MELORNE's *feet.*

ANGEL *cannot speak and* AYRE *speaks for her.* ANGEL
mimes seeking forgiveness from MELORNE.]

AYRE: 'Poor quim me am, bleak father. Forgive me,
bleak father. The 'eaven is wild. Torn a-thunder so
bad, so bad, we fain to live.'

MELORNE: [*yelling*] 'Ye child, dry quim. Ye rack o' truth
I boil, this loam boil 'cos o' me profoundest outcastin'.
[*With high emotion*] 'Outcastin'!' [*Crying at the sky*] 'Rack
'n' cat, rack 'n' cat!'

[*He jabs out both her eyes with a stick.*]

'Ye blind! Ye blind! Now, forsooth, ye can eye me pain
o' outcastin'. Ye pain goldy sow o' me tarse!'

[*He falls to the ground and sits. Singing,* MAC *covers him
with leaves and flowers.* ANGEL *plays her penny whistle.*]

MAC: [*singing*]

> Up 'n' down
> He go,
> Up 'n' down
> A-jig, jig, jig.

MELORNE: [*as though in his second childhood*] 'Bleak
outcastin', a-blub, blub, blub.'

[BETSHEB *enters.* MELORNE *spots her. They look at one
another, so ecstatic it is amusing even to the visitors,
though the actors mean it seriously. Their arms out, with
cries of delight they rush into one another's arms.*]

'True treasure o' quim 'n' tarse!'

[*They hug.*]

'Nowt more outcastin'! Nowt more!'

[*He grabs the washbasin full of gold.*]

'Joyful quim! Joyful tarse! Joyful bird! Joyful goldy sow!
Joyful day!'

[*He gives the bowl to* BETSHEB.]

'Joy o' loam.' [*Quietly*] 'Nowt more outcastin! Nowt
more.'

[*Everyone is happy.* MELORNE *leads as the company
bows to the two young men.* AYRE *applauds and*
FRANCIS *and* PETER, *who have understood very little,*

do likewise. MELORNE *takes off his top hat and joyfully runs to them, holding it out, expecting a tip. Blackout.*]

SCENE SIX

The same clearing, night. FRANCIS *and* PETER *lie on the ground talking softly. Not far away* AYRE *sits in her chair, half dozing, half listening to the night-birds.* STEF *lies at her feet,* MAC *nearby.*

PETER: [*to* FRANCIS, *looking at* AYRE] Is she sleeping?
FRANCIS: Listening.
PETER: To us?
FRANCIS: The owl.
    [AYRE *turns in the direction of a hooting owl.*]
PETER: Did you see the huts?
FRANCIS: Like those old slab squatter huts. Really primitive. God knows what happens when it rains here. Maybe they go into that cave.
PETER: It's a mine. Where their gold comes from, I suppose. That young fellow, Mac; he showed me.
    [*Silence.* AYRE *watches them, though they don't realise it.*]
FRANCIS: Well?
PETER: 'Well' what?
FRANCIS: Who do you think they are?
PETER: Maybe the play was telling us. Maybe it was their history.
    [FRANCIS *shrugs.*]
Two timbermen were discovered up north of here. They had been living alone for years. They had come to cut down Huon pine. People forgot about them but they continued to cut down the trees, though no one collected them. They were still going through the motions. They had gone mad.
    [*Suddenly* AYRE *motions to the sky, quoting loudly.*]
AYRE: 'O tell me, bird, t' where is yer goin'? O tell me,

what is yer want t' hear?' [*Smiling at the two men*] New chums. Skittle o' chance has yer to this spot, here, down in a fine ol' dark.

[*Pause.*]

I cup me ear t' the glommen bird. Soul o' the dead. Cryin' out, 'Donna burst 'er 'eart, the bird is me!' No rack 'n' cat. Heavenbirth.

[*She laughs, then sardonically motions to the hooting owl.*]

Me, moonin' in the glommen.

[*Silence.*]

[*With an all-encompassing motion of her hands*] Our goldy sow, the furst t' bloodburst int' this silent sea. Past riverrun 'n' turn o' kelp int' muddy moss, seay green 'n' here. 'Ere! Spirit eyes o' gold. In ghost time, behind us; osier 'n' 'eather 'n' 'ello, ducky. 'Oary boyos, sun-stricken girlie days. Blackysmith 'n' Trunk's Tavern. I hear the goldy lifey, the glommen lifey. Do nowt ferget dreamytime. Ferget lifey in rattlesnake, ev'ry chum cryin' to death, 'n' into 'ere, the greeny belch o' 'eaven. Danderupping so to live on the greasypole o' spirit friends. Spirits o' cunty dell. Circle o' greeny 'ome. Stars 'n' loam, firs 'n' spermy flower. Spirits, sprits, ghosts 'n' pitch dark, buboes o' the face 'n' arse 'n' ... 'n' [*motioning to* STEF *at her feet*] festerin' lip 'n' baby birdcry. Burst mouth, hairy brain 'n' cradlepain. Goldy death, goldy backward seein'. [*Motioning to her head*] Me mossy brain is the backward seein'. Pitch dark glommen is dry sheb and rottin' tarse. The circle is burst. [*Softly, almost to herself*] The circle is burst.

[*She looks at the men, hoping they have understood. Silence. She shrugs.*]

[*Looking at the sky*] I cup me ear t' the glommen bird.

[MAC *arrives, lifts* AYRE *out of the chair and helps her to walk off.* STEF, *as if startled awake, runs after them and then past them. Silence.*]

FRANCIS: Maybe she was trying to tell us what we don't know.

PETER: Perhaps.
  [PETER *stands.*]
  Nature calls.
  [*He exits.* FRANCIS *lies down, hands behind his head
  and thinks. He notices a figure. It is a curious* BETSHEB
  moving closer. FRANCIS *pretends he is sleeping. She
  moves closer.* FRANCIS *turns and faces her. She steps
  back, unsure. They stare at one another. Silence.*]
FRANCIS: The man who was dead: was he your
  husband?
  [*Pause.*]
  Was he your brother?
  [*Silence.*]
  Do you remember my name? 'Francis'.
  [*He sits up. She is frightened and hurries off into the
  night.*]
  Come back, don't be frightened.
  [*He jumps up and goes after her. Blackout.*]

SCENE SEVEN

The bush, night. FRANCIS *moves out of the moonlight and into
the shadows.* BETSHEB *enters, laughing. As* MAC *enters she
spins in her dress, around and around, making herself giddy,
and then falls on the ground. They both laugh as she tries to
stand up, but she's still too giddy. He approaches her and she
pushes him onto the ground. She pounces on him, growling
softly like an animal. She nuzzles her face into his neck: it
tickles and he laughs.* BETSHEB *jumps on him and straddles
his chest, kissing him playfully.* MAC *grows irritated and
roughly pushes her off. He tries to jump up, but her playfulness
turns to real desperation and she grabs hold of his leg. He
struggles to his feet but she holds on to him. He tries to push her
away but she won't budge. She cries like an animal in pain and
buries her face into his crotch. He hits her away; she falls to the
ground and he takes the opportunity to escape into the night.*
BETSHEB, *anguished, smashes the ground with her fists,*

moaning. FRANCIS, *shocked by what he has seen, moves into
the moonlight.* BETSHEB *doesn't notice and, weeping, jumps
up and runs off into the night.* FRANCIS *stands where he is,
trying to make sense of what he has seen and the extraordinary
primal agony and passion of* BETSHEB. *As he stands thinking
night gives way to dawn.* PETER *enters.*

PETER: Where did you get to last night?
[FRANCIS *starts from his preoccupation.*]
You look awful.
FRANCIS: I couldn't sleep.
PETER: The old geezer got me up. Took me into the
mine. I think he realises I know something about
rocks. I didn't know if he wanted my advice or to show
off. I tried to explain that the damn thing would cave
in. You should see it, it's bloody primitive:
water-logged, a few struts. We'd better get started
back soon.
[*Pause.*]
Did you hear?
[FRANCIS *nods.*]
What's the matter?
FRANCIS: Nothing.
PETER: Something's bothering you.
FRANCIS: I want to find out who they are.
[BETSHEB *brings in* AYRE's *chair.* FRANCIS *catches her
eye as* AYRE *comes out helped by* ANGEL. AYRE *looks
more infirm than on the previous night.*]
[*To* BETSHEB] Last night I saw you down near the river.
[BETSHEB *doesn't understand.*]
AYRE: [*sitting in her chair and looking at the sky*] Sun, sun,
sun, sun. Jack straw, barley o' life. Eh?
[*She basks her face in the morning sun and dozes.* MAC
enters and looks at BETSHEB. *They are awkward and
embarrassed about what happened the night before.
Suddenly, seemingly from nowhere,* MELORNE *runs in
and knocks* MAC *down.* MELORNE *circles* MAC, *smiling
broadly, urging him to wrestle.* MAC *doesn't want to
fight.*]
PETER: [*to* FRANCIS] He's crazy about wrestling, wants to

prove himself. When we came out of the mine he jumped on me, wanting to wrestle.

FRANCIS: Did you?

PETER: A bloody fit old bugger; he soon had me giving up.

FRANCIS: [*to* MELORNE, *calling*] Here!

[MELORNE *turns around.*]

PETER: What are you doing? He's crazy.

FRANCIS: I want to see how good he is.

[*The old man laughs. He loves wrestling.*]

[*To* MELORNE] Mad as a hatter, aren't you?

[MELORNE *nods and smiles broadly.*]

I can see it in your eyes.

PETER: Careful, he's quick.

[*But just as* PETER *warns* FRANCIS, MELORNE *leaps at him and knocks him down.* FRANCIS *quickly pushes him off and jumps up.*]

FRANCIS: [*to* PETER] He's bloody quick. Strong too.

[*Smiling at* MELORNE] Do that again.

[MELORNE *takes a step towards* FRANCIS. *The younger man jumps him. They wrestle on the ground. Everyone is enthralled by the contest. It quickly turns from a lighthearted game into something deadly serious:* FRANCIS, *like* MELORNE, *is not the type to give in. Advantage goes one way and then the other.* MELORNE *jumps up,* FRANCIS *moves towards him. The old man spits at him viciously.* FRANCIS *decides to thrash* MELORNE *now. He lunges at the old man, there is a vicious series of grabs, tackles and falls.* MELORNE *tires and pulls away.* PETER *realises that* MELORNE *is beaten and also knows that* FRANCIS *is angry enough to do serious injury.*]

PETER: Leave him alone, Francis. You've won. You've beaten him.

FRANCIS: [*keeping his eyes on* MELORNE] No I haven't. Not yet. I'm going to crush him.

[*He moves in on* MELORNE. *They circle one another.* FRANCIS *suddenly dives on the older man, throwing him to the ground and lands on him heavily. He forces the old*

man into a position of defeat and pain. MELORNE *cries
out in anguish.*]
[*Yelling*] Give up!
PETER: [*going to him*] You've defeated him. Come on.
FRANCIS: [*to* MELORNE, *angrily*] Give up.
PETER: [*grabbing him*] Francis! [*Pulling him away*] For
Christ's sake, you could kill him.
FRANCIS: That's what he wanted to do to me.
[MAC *and* ANGEL *go to* MELORNE *and lift him up.*]
PETER: What were you trying to prove?
FRANCIS: [*calming down*] He just seemed to be asking for
it. It's the only thing he understands.
PETER: The same would apply to you, it would seem.
[MELORNE *angrily shrugs off* ANGEL *and* MAC *and
walks over to* FRANCIS. *The two men stare at one
another.* FRANCIS *is apprehensive.* MELORNE *abruptly
thrusts out his hand.* FRANCIS *and* PETER *flinch, but he
only wants to shake hands with the victor. Everyone
applauds.*]

SCENE EIGHT

The river, twilight. BETSHEB *sits, staring out at the evening
sun. Near her feet are flowers she has just picked. She hums a
tune to herself. Nearby,* STEF *rolls on the ground, laughing to
himself.* FRANCIS *enters and watches* BETSHEB *for some time.*

FRANCIS: Are you looking at the sunset?
[*Startled,* BETSHEB *turns around.*]
[*Smiling*] I'm not a monster ... No more running.
[*Silence. He walks closer to the river.*]
Look at us reflected in the water, see? Upside-down.
[*He smiles and she smiles back. Silence.*]
So quiet. I'm not used to such silence. I'm a city boy,
born and bred. You've never seen a city or town, have
you? Where I live there are dozens of factories: shoe
factories, some that make gaskets, hydraulic

machines, clothing. My mother works in a shoe factory. [*Pointing to his boots*] These came from my mother's factory.

[*Silence.*]

These sunsets here, I've never seen the likes of them. A bit of muddy orange light in the distance, behind the chimneys, is generally all I get to see.

[*Pause.*]

You'd like the trams, especially at night. They rattle and squeak, like ghosts rattling their chains, and every so often the conducting rod hits a terminus and there is a brilliant spark of electricity, like an axe striking a rock. 'Spisss!' On Saturday afternoon thousands of people go and watch the football. A huge oval of grass. [*Miming a football*] A ball like this. Someone hand passes it, 'whish', straight to me. I duck one lumbering giant, spin around a nifty dwarf of a rover, then I catch sight of the goals. I boot a seventy-yard drop kick straight through the centre. The crowd goes wild!

[*He cheers wildly.* BETSHEB *laughs at his actions. He is pleased to have made her laugh.*]

Not as good as your play.

[*Pause.*]

This is your home. My home is across the water, Bass Strait.

[*Silence.* STEF *rolls over and ends up near* FRANCIS' *feet.*]

What is it about you people? Why are you like you are?

[BETSHEB *gathers up her flowers. As she stands she drops a few.*]

Don't go.

[*He picks up the fallen flowers.*]

I was watching you pick these. My mother steals flowers from her neighbour's front garden so every morning she can have fresh flowers in her vase for Saint Teresa's portrait. She was a woman centuries ago. God fired a burning arrow of love into her. [*Smiling*] When it penetrated her, Saint Teresa could smell the burning flesh of her heart.

[BETSHEB *does a parody of the wrestling match, but to her it is so funny that she cannot go on.* FRANCIS *smiles uncertainly.* STEF *crawls across the ground, growling to himself, then sits and rocks back and forth, staring into the distance.*]

BETSHEB: [*to* FRANCIS, *with a very thick accent*] Stef 'ave cradlepain.
[*She strokes* STEF's *head.*]
[*Murmuring*] Stef, Stef, Stef, Stef. [*In a sing-song voice*] Sha' it up, dee, dee, dee.

FRANCIS: You can actually talk ... talk like the old lady. Like Ayre.
[*She looks closely at* FRANCIS.]
Talk. You can talk like Ayre.
[BETSHEB *is unsure what he's talking about.* STEF *begins to move away;* BETSHEB *follows and helps him.* PETER *arrives unnoticed and watches* FRANCIS *watching* BETSHEB *and* STEF. *The couple leaves.* FRANCIS *picks up a few pebbles and starts to skim them across the river.*]

PETER: It rose last night.
[FRANCIS *turns, momentarily startled.*]
FRANCIS: Imagine how this place is in winter.
PETER: How many times can you get them to skip?
FRANCIS: Four or five.
PETER: I could never do it.
FRANCIS: Used to go down to the Yarra near Dight Falls and practice.
[*Silence.*]
PETER: Is she the reason you want to stay?
FRANCIS: I want to find out about these people.
PETER: What attracts you to her?
FRANCIS: She's interesting, in a way.
PETER: It's because you don't know anything about her. She's probably as crazy as the rest of them.
FRANCIS: They're not crazy.
PETER: My father would certify them.
[*Pause.*]
I had a closer look at that wash basin. There's no gold

in it, just quartz, a bit of copper, alum, iron pyrites ...
Fool's gold. I had a look over the back there too.
There used to be other houses, a long time ago. And
another mine.
[*Pause.*]
FRANCIS: How's the old fellow?
PETER: Coughing up blood.
FRANCIS: You think he'll die?
[*Silence.*]
PETER: It wasn't your fault.
[*Silence.*]
We'll head back tomorrow morning?
[FRANCIS *nods.*]
We'll get some experts out here; they'll find out what
this is all about.
[*Pause.*]
FRANCIS: She can't understand me, or at least I think she
doesn't, but I know she's absorbing it like a sponge,
soaking up what I'm saying. I see her listening to Ayre,
you know, when they're together and it is as if she's
soaking up all that Ayre is telling her. Remembering.
Recording.
PETER: Check your knapsack; someone's been through
it.
[*He exits.* FRANCIS *returns to skimming pebbles across
the surface of the river.*]

SCENE NINE

The bush, night. Clouds obscure the moon. BETSHEB *is
perched on* MAC'*s shoulders. They turn slowly on the spot like
a ballerina on a music box. From a distance* ANGEL'*s penny
whistle plays a haunting tune. The whole thing has a distant
dream-like feel, almost like a memory.* BETSHEB *stares up at
the sky.*

BETSHEB: [*murmuring softly*]

> Rain, rain, go thy way,
> Come a-back ne'er a day ...

[*She repeats this incantation over and over. The lights fade and come up again.*]

SCENE TEN

The bush, night. Thunder sounds. AYRE *sits in her chair, a beautiful, unworn 1850s dress on her lap. She looks up at the thunder and clouds. Something is preying on her mind. She tries to remember a song.*

AYRE: 'Little Peggy ...' 'Peggy ...' 'She met 'im in ...'
   [*She can't remember it. She looks down at the dress and strokes it like a lap dog.*]
'Airloomin' fer the child. Wot child? Bellsademon laughin'. Nowt need nowt Herod. We is dead. Goldy dead nowt goldy sow. Nowt tongue, nowt goldy sow, nowt 'istory.
   [*Silence. She feels the beautiful material of the dress.*]
So fine. So fine. 'I shew yer beauty. Beauty so fine yer'll piss yerself. 'Airloomin' fer the child.'
   [*Silence. She comes to a decision.*]
Nowt more outcastin'. [*Crying out to the sky*] Nowt more outcastin'!

SCENE ELEVEN

The bush, night. BETSHEB *sits alone on the ground and examines the contents of a rough cloth bag.* FRANCIS *enters and watches her surreptitiously. She takes out and examines a watch, then a book and then a small compass; finally she takes out a large lizard. She stares at it intently and hisses at it, her tongue flicking in and out at it. She seems mightily intrigued by this reptile.*

FRANCIS: [*quietly*] Betsheb.
  [BETSHEB *doesn't turn around. She seems to have already known* FRANCIS *was nearby. She puts the lizard back in the cloth bag.*]
BETSHEB: [*quietly, almost to herself*] Francis.
  [*He comes over and sits down beside her.*]
FRANCIS: I couldn't sleep.
  [*Silence.* FRANCIS *notices the objects.*]
  These are mine. [*Picking up the watch*] A watch. [*Winding it*] It tells the time, tells us how old we're getting.
  [*He holds it to her ear.*]
  See? Can you hear it? 'Tick, tick, tick', like a heartbeat.
  [*He picks up the compass.*]
  Compass. See the arrow? [*Indicating*] North is that way. Somewhere that way is Hobart. [*Sardonically*] Somewhere. And this ... this is a book.
  [*She nods as if she knows.*]
  The Structure of Single Span Bridges.
BETSHEB: Book.
FRANCIS: You know it's a book?
  [*She nods.*]
BETSHEB: [*pretending to read, turning the pages quickly*] Thy word.
  [BETSHEB *stands and motions to the sky.*]

  (Rain, rain, go thy way,
  Come a-back ne'er a day.

'Ate the olcer sky. No end. No end. Adorate the shiny brocade sky, glommen time. Queenie Ayre say in ancient glommen, King David see the brocade, King Moses see the goldy brocade, lubilashings o' shiny in ancient glommen. The sky 'e see, is me goldy brocade. See?
  [*She stands and spins slowly, staring up at the sky as if*

intoxicated by it and her words. We hear distant thunder.]

FRANCIS: The last waltz, *madame.*

[*He grabs her. She starts as if woken from an intense reverie.*]

Dance. Dancing. Follow me. Arm here. [*Singing a waltz melody*] Da, da, da ... That's right, that's right, turn here, now a step here ... Right ...

[*She quickly picks it up.*]

My mother forced me to learn dancing so I would be able to mix in the proper circles at university.

[*Suddenly he kisses her. She tries to pull away.*]

No!

[*He holds on to her roughly and kisses her again. She bites him on the lip. He grimaces in pain. She pulls away.* FRANCIS *puts a finger to his lips and spots blood on it.* BETSHEB *is apprehensive.*]

I only wanted to kiss you.

[*Pause.*]

You do it with Mac, why not with me?

[*Silence.*]

I want to break through to you and I don't know how. I don't even know if you're stupid or crazy or whatever.

[*He walks towards her.*]

Don't run away. [*Smiling*] I can smell my heart burning.

[*She moves towards him and presses her forehead tightly against his.*]

BETSHEB: Me burstin' brain. Me burstin' brain. See?

[*He doesn't understand.*]

FRANCIS: You're hurting.

[*But she desperately wants him to understand.*]

BETSHEB: Break 'n' crack int' thee.

[*She abruptly pulls away and looks at the sky, disappointed by* FRANCIS' *lack of understanding. There is a loud roll of thunder.*]

(Rain, rain, go thy way,

Come a-back ne'er a day.

[*She takes* FRANCIS' *hand and kisses it. She then takes a small cardboard-backed photograph from between her breasts and gives it to him.*]

FRANCIS: A photograph. Is this woman your mother?

BETSHEB: Ghost o' me flesh.

FRANCIS: Grandmother?

[BETSHEB *points to something in the photograph.*]

Painted backdrop. Photographer's studio. That's not a real mountain or waterfall.

[*She points to something else, then touches her dress.*]

Yes, it's like your dress. Well, when it was new. Is it yours?

[BETSHEB *pays no attention to his question. She takes the photograph, kisses it, then puts it inside her dress. She is ecstatic. She runs up the river bank, turns and throws herself on the ground and rolls over and over down to him like a log rolling down a hill, then jumps up, pretending to be* MELORNE *asking for his hat to take up a collection.* FRANCIS *laughs at her imitation.* BETSHEB *then squats and pretends to piss, making groaning, pissing noises; a broad grin of contentment passes over her face. She does a parody of a high-born woman. She pretends to sit and sip tea at an exclusive dinner party. She speaks as if delivering bon mots to imaginary guests.*]

BETSHEB: Shit, shit, shit, shit, shit.

[FRANCIS *laughs at her slightly bitter parody.*]

FRANCIS: Lady So-And-So's tea party?

[BETSHEB *is extremely happy showing off to* FRANCIS. *She prowls around him like a wild, vicious dog sniffing its prey, and then she turns into a snarling, spitting Tasmanian devil, an act which slightly unnerves* FRANCIS. *Abruptly, she changes again and begins to walk like a grande dame taking a promenade. She motions to convicts nearby and gives them orders.*]

BETSHEB: Rack 'n' cat, rack 'n' cat, rack 'n' cat, rack 'n' cat.

[*Then the grande dame farts. She discretely waves her*

hand behind her to get rid of the smell. FRANCIS *laughs at the parody.*]

FRANCIS: Where did you pick that up from? Ayre? Did Ayre teach you?

BETSHEB *pays no attention to him. She crawls over to him, tongue flicking in and out like a lizard's. She kisses him on the mouth with her flickering tongue.*]

BETSHEB: Bellsademon kissin' 'n' spoonkissin' in the rye. [*Murmuring*] The belle she lie droopin'. The gent he lie tongue out. Ho! Spoonfuckin' in the glommen.

[*She lifts her dress and sits down.*]

FRANCIS: Are you sure?

[*He sits down next to her.*]

BETSHEB: [*smiling, softly*] The belle whoopin', tongue out in the glommen.

[*They kiss.*]

FRANCIS: [*feeling her flesh*] Soft. So soft.

[*He kisses her on the lips again. The thunder comes closer, but they pay no attention to it. He kisses her on the inside of her legs. She ruffles his hair as if he were a dog. He takes off his shirt, then kisses her again. The whole of her body begins to tremble violently, as if possessed by involuntary muscle spasms. She lashes out and tears at her clothes. Her eyes roll, her body convulses. It is like an epileptic fit.*]

[*Concerned*] Betsheb!

[*He tries to hold her, to calm her, but her body is uncontrollable. She lashes out, without knowing what she is doing, and hits him.*]

Betsheb ... Betsheb ... What is it? Please ... Do you want me to get help? [*Crying out*] Peter!

[*She begins to calm down. He strokes her as if soothing a child.*]

That's right ... [*Soothingly*] Calm. Calm down.

[*She is still, silent.*]

I'm sorry.

[*Silence. He holds her in his arms. Suddenly she wakes as if from a nightmare. Horrified she realises she has blacked out. She looks at her clothes and wipes away the*

saliva that has formed around the edges of her mouth.
Now that she realises what she's done she is ashamed. She
jumps up and away from him.]
BETSHEB: No, no, no ...
FRANCIS: It's all right, it's over.
[*She is angry with her body. She starts to tear at it, then*
motions to her head as if to say she is stupid. She spits on
her body because it has betrayed her. FRANCIS *comes over*
to her, but she pushes him away, humiliated.]
BETSHEB: Go, go!
[*Pause.*]
FRANCIS: You want me to go away? [*Motioning*] You want
me to leave you? It's nothing to be ashamed of.
BETSHEB: [*pushing him away*] Go. Go.
FRANCIS: Will you be all right?
BETSHEB: Thee, way! Go! [*Picking up a stone and throwing*
it at him] Go!
[FRANCIS *reluctantly moves away. She sinks to the*
ground with her back to him, exhausted. FRANCIS *sits*
also, far away from her, and watches. The thunder comes
closer.]
FRANCIS: It is going to pour. You should go in.
[*Silence.*]
Let's go in.
[*Silence.*]
Talk to me.
[*Silence. Despondent,* BETSHEB *lies on the ground.*
Scattered before her are the three objects she stole from
FRANCIS' *knapsack.* FRANCIS *stares at the violent sky.*
BETSHEB *stares at the objects with distant eyes. As she*
stares they move towards her, one by one, slowly and
firmly, as though by telekinesis. The watch is first to move
along the ground, then the compass, then the book. She
makes no move to gather them as they stop in front of her.
FRANCIS *sees none of this.*]
BETSHEB: [*to herself, quietly*] Francis.
PETER: [*off, calling*] Francis.
[FRANCIS *stands up.* PETER *enters. Close behind him*
MAC *carries* MELORNE. BETSHEB *retreats*

apprehensively. MAC *puts* MELORNE *on the ground and
lays him out. As he does so,* STEF *enters and sits down to
play with the compass.*]
He's dying.

FRANCIS: Why bring him here? A storm's coming.

PETER: He wants to die outside.

[FRANCIS *is reluctant to come closer.* ANGEL *enters with
a large, battered box which she puts down.*]
Come closer. He knows it wasn't your fault. He wanted
to come to you.

[FRANCIS *moves closer, then drops to his knees.*]

FRANCIS: Sorry, old man.

[MELORNE'*s hand suddenly snakes out and grabs*
FRANCIS'. *He squeezes it tightly.* FRANCIS *is afraid.*
MELORNE *grunts with exertion as if wrestling, then
laughs triumphantly. The effort has been too much; he
sinks back.* ANGEL *hurries over to him.* AYRE *enters
slowly and painfully.* MELORNE *tries to cry out but
cannot.* ANGEL *holds his hand. He smiles at her and
dies.* ANGEL *tries to call to him, but like a baby can only
get out the first part of 'Daddy'.*]

ANGEL: D-d-d-d- ...

[*Silence.* ANGEL *silently hugs the dead* MELORNE.]

AYRE: [*to* FRANCIS *and* PETER] The circle is burst. We is
burstin' int' the glommen. Outburst. Bellsademon
land; cradlepain. Circle is burst. Nowt more
outcastin'. Nowt more sin fer bread.

[AYRE *gives* MAC *a signal and he opens the box.*]
See!

[*The two young men look inside the box.*]
Goldy sow o' the 'airloomin' pit.

[FRANCIS *takes out the doll seen before.*]
Sa, Sa.

[*He takes out the dress seen earlier.*]
Promin'. 'Airloomin'.

[*He takes out the book.*]

FRANCIS: What is it?

PETER: The writing's too faint to see.

AYRE: [*motioning to the distance*] Way! Way!

PETER: She's telling us to go.
   [FRANCIS *suddenly realises.*]
FRANCIS: No, this is their luggage, their belongings.
AYRE: Nowt more outcastin'. Nowt more outcastin'.
FRANCIS: She wants us to take them back with us. You
   want to go back with us, Ayre?
AYRE: Yea.
   [*Silence. The storm breaks.* AYRE *looks at the
   grief-stricken* ANGEL *as she cradles* MELORNE.]
   Nowt more outcastin'. Nowt more outcastin' ...

SCENE TWELVE

---

*The Archers' garden, twilight. It is a warm evening. In the
background is the Greek temple. A long table with an expensive
setting is ready: porcelain crockery, silverware and crystal
glasses; food is on the table.* ELIZABETH *escorts* GEORGE
ROSS, *Federal M.P., into the garden.*

ELIZABETH: It was such a lovely evening we decided to
   have it out here. We expected you later.
GEORGE: The Cabinet meeting took less time than I
   thought.
ELIZABETH: They won't be long.
GEORGE: I'm most intrigued to see them. Your husband's
   report was extraordinary.
   [*He notices the Greek temple.*]
   Not many of those in Australian backyards.
ELIZABETH: It was built way back in eighteen forty —
   only Australians could say 'way back in eighteen forty'
   — by my grandfather. He loved Greece, Greek
   culture; a family trait. So he built this little Olympus.
   It was said that he had a giant streak of paganism in his
   soul. The architect, an ex-convict, unfortunately used
   poor materials. It took the Parthenon two thousand
   years to crumble; it took our temple less than a
   hundred. Occasionally I let the spirits of the Greeks

take hold of me and I put on an ancient tragedy. Once we performed *Iphigenia in Tauris* to help a charity for unwed mothers and, do you know, some people looked down on us. But being an unwed mother is so human: one moment of passion, a lifetime of misery. Years ago, William and I could have said those speeches in ancient Greek and most of the audience would have understood; many of them were academics and artists, of course. That was our greatest period of civilisation. From then on it's been all downhill. Romans conquered the world and Mussolini takes years to conquer a few Ethiopian hill tribes. Ah, who are these handsome young men?

> [PETER *and* FRANCIS *enter wearing tuxedos.* FRANCIS *is agitated.*]

Mr Ross, I would like to introduce my son, Peter. Peter, this is Mr George Ross, Federal Minister for Health.

PETER: [*shaking hands*] How do you do, sir?

ELIZABETH: And his friend, Francis Morris.

GEORGE: Very glad to meet you.

> [*They shake hands.*]

ELIZABETH: Francis's fascination with these people is only matched by my husband's.

GEORGE: Doctor Archer's report mentioned you two found this group. I couldn't not come, my curiosity about them was too great.

ELIZABETH: This will be the first time you've seen them since you brought them back, won't it?

FRANCIS: Yes.

> [PETER *pours* FRANCIS *a glass of wine to try and calm him.*]

GEORGE: [*looking around*] And this is where they've been staying?

ELIZABETH: William thought they would be more comfortable here and it would make studying them easier. The woman, Angel, is in hospital, however. She has pulmonary tuberculosis. Her brother, Mac, is with her; it's thought he may have a touch of it too.

GEORGE: So they won't be coming tonight?

ELIZABETH: No. How was Melbourne, Francis? Francis?

[FRANCIS *sips his glass of wine. For a moment he is at a loss.*]

The job?

FRANCIS: I didn't get it.

ELIZABETH: Perhaps next time. Have you heard the latest about Poland, Mr Ross?

GEORGE: They say Poland is about to surrender.

ELIZABETH: I can feel it in my blood. Another world war. The times are definitely out of joint. And, again, we'll send our youth off to die.

GEORGE: If it's necessary to fight Nazism. Would you sign up, Francis?

FRANCIS: Yes. Fascism has to be destroyed; it's an evil philosophy. If I had been older I would have fought against it in Spain.

GEORGE: [*amused*] Oh, an idealist.

ELIZABETH: [*looking off*] Ah, here they are.

[*It is an extraordinary sight.* BETSHEB *and* AYRE *are dressed magnificently.* AYRE *wears the dress she held in her lap and* BETSHEB *wears a modern evening dress.* STEF *wears a dinner jacket. They are escorted by* WILLIAM, *also dressed in a dinner jacket.* STEF *shambles stiffly to the table, attracted by the glitter and the candles.* BETSHEB *guides* AYRE *in. Both women stop when they see* FRANCIS *and* PETER. *They are pleased to see both.*]

WILLIAM: [*to* BETSHEB] Here, I'll take Queenie Ayre.

[WILLIAM *leads* AYRE *to the central chair.* BETSHEB *and* FRANCIS *stare shyly at one another.*]

BETSHEB: 'Ello.

FRANCIS: Hello.

ELIZABETH: My, how wonderful you look.

FRANCIS: You look lovely.

[BETSHEB *spins in her dress for everyone, delighted by the praise. She stops and smiles at* FRANCIS.]

BETSHEB: [*quietly*] The belle is spoonin'.
[STEF *puts his hand into one of the dips. He tastes it, then spits it out in horror.*]
WILLIAM: Mr Ross, I'm Doctor Archer.
GEORGE: Of course, I remember you well; that conference last year.
[STEF *sits on the grass and rocks back and forth, humming to himself.*]
WILLIAM: Actually, in only a week Stef has improved out of sight.
GEORGE: Did you find out who they are?
WILLIAM: These people are the last members of a group that goes back to the eighteen fifties, during the gold rushes when everyone had the fever. Bankers, convicts, businessmen, doctors ... but unlike in Victoria, the rush finished pretty quickly here. One group moved much further into the South West looking for gold than anyone else. Most of them were ex-convicts, escaped convicts, failed colonists, general scum ... even a travelling actor tired of doing bad shows for stupid colonists. One of the escaped convicts by the name of 'Simpson' kept a notebook. Some of it is his information, but the rest of the notebook is his obsession with his dreams. He dreamed he should found his own town, independent of the rest of mankind, so he tried to. And what material did he have? Criminals, retards, the lost, the desperate. [*Smiling*] So what we have before us is the true Australian culture.
GEORGE: What about the way they talk?
WILLIAM: Simpson, like his sister, had a cleft palate. Their language is a word salad made up of Cockney, Scottish, Irish dialects. There must have been a thread of retardation running through the original group because some of them just didn't learn to speak.
FRANCIS: Perhaps they didn't feel the need to speak.
WILLIAM: [*amused*] Of the younger ones, only Betsheb can talk. Ayre forces her to. Once Ayre dies, Betsheb will be the last repository of their culture. Stef is

Angel's son; he's the final genetic mockery. Betsheb's brother died recently.

FRANCIS: The corpse?

WILLIAM: Yes. And Mac will never be able to have children because his genitals are malformed. Queenie Ayre is a woman I admire more each day. It would have taken a lot of courage to come back to the world of 'rack 'n' cat'. Back to the world she had only heard about, a world of racks, whips, prison, hatred. She knows they have no future in the wilderness. Inside her head she has kept everything she deems important. Dreams, memories, snatches of songs, Bible stories ... it's had to be passed on by word of mouth.

[*Silence. The three newcomers look curiously vulnerable and* BETSHEB *and* AYRE *are embarrassed as the others stare at them.* STEF, *stares at the sky.*]

FRANCIS: What's going to happen to them?

WILLIAM: We decided not to let the public know until we know a little more about them. [*Looking at* GEORGE] We plan to release the information on Tuesday.

[GEORGE *nods.*]

So, ladies and gentlemen, the children of our past.

[AYRE *points to* ELIZABETH]

ELIZABETH: What is it, Ayre?

AYRE: [*motioning to* ELIZABETH's *neck*] Shiny, shiny.

[ELIZABETH *takes off the necklace and gives it to her.*]

ELIZABETH: For tonight.

[*She puts it around* AYRE's *neck.* AYRE *is very pleased.* PETER *sits down to have a drink.* WILLIAM *pours one for* GEORGE. WILLIAM *watches as* FRANCIS *approaches* BETSHEB. STEF *begins to stalk* GEORGE.]

FRANCIS: You wear your dress with more ease than I wear this monkey suit.

BETSHEB: I look fer thee, dawnytime, day fer day.

WILLIAM: 'I looked for you every morning, day after day.'

BETSHEB: I nowt more a-feared.

WILLIAM: 'I'm not afraid any more.'

FRANCIS: [*to* WILLIAM] I know.
[*A broad smile crosses* BETSHEB's *face as she remembers something.*]
BETSHEB: I see car ...
[WILLIAM *translates, proud of his skill and also realising that when* BETSHEB *gets excited she is hard to understand.*]
WILLIAM: 'I was in a car.'
BETSHEB: Windwhistlin'.
WILLIAM: 'It went quickly.'
BETSHEB: 'Ome, country groan 'n' moan 'n' run.
WILLIAM: 'Factories and houses make noises and the landscape from the car makes it look like it's running.'
BETSHEB: Voice in a stick.
WILLIAM: 'Telephone.' She loves hearing people speak on the telephone.
BETSHEB: I laugh. Let go.
[*She demonstrates listening on the telephone.*]
Demon or 'eaven?
WILLIAM: 'The voices, are they from heaven or hell?'
[STEF *pounces on* GEORGE *and starts to chew his ankle, growling.*]
WILLIAM: Pay no attention.
GEORGE: [*thin-lipped*] I'll try.
ELIZABETH: Shall we sit? Francis, you escort Betsheb.
[GEORGE *pretends not to notice as* STEF *clings by his teeth to* GEORGE's *trousers. He makes his awkward way to the table.* BETSHEB *is highly excited at meeting* FRANCIS *again.* WILLIAM *pulls* STEF *free of* GEORGE's *trousers.*]
GEORGE: Much appreciated, Doctor Archer.
[WILLIAM *sits* STEF *at the table.* BETSHEB *suddenly cries out like a magpie. Everyone looks at her. Now that she has their attention she decides to show off. She remembers how* FRANCIS *enjoyed her performance down by the river, so she steps away and begins to promenade like a grande dame.*]
BETSHEB: Rack 'n' cat, rack 'n' cat, rack 'n' cat ...
[*She turns around for her return walk.* FRANCIS *realises what will come next.*]

FRANCIS: [*horrified*] Betsheb!

> [*But* BETSHEB *doesn't hear him. She farts loudly, much to* AYRE's *amusement, and pretends discreetly to wave the smell away. She notices that no one else is laughing. She is suddenly worried.*]

ELIZABETH: [*to* WILLIAM] You couldn't get anything more Australian than that! [*To* BETSHEB] Bravo, Betsheb! [*Applauding*] Bravo!

> [*The others applaud.* BETSHEB *is pleased.* STEF *is fascinated by the candles, especially the one near him. He blows it out.*]

[*To* WILLIAM] The matches.

GEORGE: Allow me, Mrs Archer.

> [GEORGE *takes out his matches and relights the candle.* STEF *blows it out again: he enjoys this game.*]

ELIZABETH: I think, Mr Ross, that shifting the candle might save an enormous match bill.

GEORGE: I think you may be right, Mrs Archer.

> [GEORGE *shifts the candle.* STEF *is very annoyed and lunges across the table at it, scattering plates and glasses everywhere. He grabs the candle and sinks back in his chair, holding it inches from his face. He stares at its flame as if mesmerised by it.* GEORGE *goes to take the candle from him but the boy growls at him.*]

ELIZABETH: For your own safety, Minister, I suggest you let Stef keep it.

> [GEORGE *does so.* WILLIAM *pours the champagne.*]

WILLIAM: I thought we might make a toast to our visitors.

> [BETSHEB *goes to drink her champagne.*]

FRANCIS: Betsheb ... not yet.

> [AYRE *takes hers and gulps it down.* BETSHEB *sees her and follows suit.*]

ELIZABETH: I suppose a queen is entitled to invent her own table manners.

> [*She indicates to* WILLIAM *that he should pour more champagne for the women.*]

[*As he sets down the bottle*] William, short and sweet before it's too late.

> [WILLIAM *raises his glass and, with the exception of*]

STEF, *the others do likewise.* AYRE *and* BETSHEB *raise
their glasses, curious as to the meaning of this ritual.*]
WILLIAM: To our five aliens who have landed on this
strange planet, no longer called Van Diemen's Land,
but Tasmania, and to their queen, Queenie Ayre.
OTHERS: Queenie Ayre.
[STEF *stares at the candle.* AYRE *downs her glass
quickly. The others sip theirs,* BETSHEB *carefully
imitating* FRANCIS.]

SCENE THIRTEEN

The Archer's garden, night. The meal has been eaten and only
STEF *is left, lying on the grass playing with a candle.* GEORGE
and WILLIAM *enter from the garden.* STEF *secretly stalks
them.*

GEORGE: It must need a lot of gardeners.
WILLIAM: Two full-time, one part-time. It's modelled
after Beckford's classical English garden, Fonthill.
[*They stop and watch* STEF, *who pretends to look at the
candle.*]
GEORGE: You picked up their language very quickly. I
find it a real pea soup.
WILLIAM: I wouldn't leave them alone. Drove them mad,
trying to understand it.
GEORGE: [*touching* STEF *with his foot*] Doesn't notice much
about him, does he?
WILLIAM: It's hard to know.
GEORGE: Asylum patients make me feel the same way.
They seem unfathomable. As if they could do
anything.
[*Pause.*]
As you can well appreciate, Doctor Archer, with
Australia now at war the Government has many
important things on its mind. Our primary aim will be
to help defeat the Germans. Have you read any of the

Nazi philosophy? Foul. A cesspool of human hatred.

[STEF *is intrigued by* GEORGE'*s trouser legs and watches like a dog observing its prey.*]

The Cabinet decided I should take care of this matter as I have medical experience myself. You know it's going to be a very popular piece in the newspapers here and overseas? That would be true to say, wouldn't it?

[STEF *pounces on* GEORGE'*s leg and sinks his teeth in.*]

WILLIAM: Stef! Stef! Let go!

[WILLIAM *pulls him off.*]

GEORGE: Does he always do that?

WILLIAM: He likes to pretend he's our corgi.

[STEF *rocks back and forth and laughs at some huge private joke.*]

GEORGE: You realise the fuss these people are going to cause?

[WILLIAM *nods.*]

Isn't there an asylum not far from here?

WILLIAM: New Norfolk.

GEORGE: That's the one. I visited it once. Quite nice. I'll look at it again in the morning.

WILLIAM: I don't quite understand.

GEORGE: Do you want it plainer?

WILLIAM: These people aren't mad.

GEORGE: The Cabinet has decided that the public is not to know about these people until the war is over.

WILLIAM: But why? They're not mad!

GEORGE: Now listen to me. In Germany Stef would have been put to death a long time ago. The basis of Nazism is that there is a pure Aryan race and it must be kept free from impure bloodlines or genetic faults. Since they have come to power they have systematically murdered the retarded and deformed. Imagine the glee with which the Germans would greet the news that it only took three generations to result in someone like Stef. What a coup for Nazi propaganda. They would be proved right. Once the war is over, then we'll allow the public to know about them.

WILLIAM: You can't do this. They didn't come back to
civilisation to be put into an asylum.

GEORGE: These people should not be seen as examples of
the correctness of Nazi beliefs.

WILLIAM: But you'll prove it! You've demonstrated they
are right by locking these people up ...

GEORGE: This is war, Archer. I'm saying that the Nazis
will bend, reshape the information for their own
purposes. These people cannot be seen to be an
endorsement of Nazi beliefs.

[*Pause.*]

Can't you see the Government's position?

WILLIAM: I don't have much choice, do I?

GEORGE: No.

[STEF *rolls around making wind noises.* GEORGE *stares
at him.*]

You know, in some ways the Nazis are right. It took
only three generations to get to him, only three
generations to lose a language, the power to speak.
They are a genetic graveyard.

[*Pause.*]

I must get back to my hotel. Tomorrow will be hectic.

WILLIAM: I'll phone for a taxi.

[*They walk off in silence.* BETSHEB *and* FRANCIS *enter
happily from the garden.*]

FRANCIS: And is that your favourite spot?

BETSHEB: I eye the skyey blue 'n' call t' yer. Call 'n' call
'n' yer come.

[*He takes her by the waist and they dance to distant piano
music.* ELIZABETH *enters.*]

ELIZABETH: There you are. Don't you want to come in
and watch Mr Turner play? He came especially.

FRANCIS: We can hear it out here.

ELIZABETH: If Mr Turner hadn't been born blind he
would have been a great pianist. She missed you. Every
morning she asked William where you were. He, as
you know, has become quite, quite fascinated by them.

[*She picks up a wine glass and sips from it.*]

Tipsy. It's as if the dead have come alive. Ghosts from

the nether world of an Australian childhood.

[*The piano stops.* BETSHEB *steps away and goes into the garden near the temple steps.*]

There are rumours that William refused to allow other doctors to see them; that he kept them to himself, as if they were prize exhibits that no one else could look at. For twenty-four hours a day he lives and breathes them.

[BETSHEB *squats unselfconsciously and pisses.*]

They are not children, Francis, and they are not adults; they are a poor contaminated people.

FRANCIS: I think I can look after myself, Mrs Archer.

ELIZABETH: Can you? I see her early in the morning, from my window, lying on the lawn, stroking herself as if she has some invisible lover; and she talks to herself or to the sky, I don't know which. At such times I doubt her sanity.

[*The piano starts again.*]

When the news of this group breaks I will lose William. They will be his, he will explain them, he will make us understand them. Best I go inside. Mr Turner becomes quite put off by Queenie Ayre's snoring.

[*Looking at the temple, smiling*] I remember the day before you and Peter left for your trip. I was Iphigenia bemoaning my fate. As I looked down from the temple steps I saw such an expression of horror on your face, a look of 'What sort of world is Peter's?'

[*She laughs.* FRANCIS *smiles.*]

They'll change too. All the publicity, all the attention. Then we'll lose them.

[*She exits.* BETSHEB *shivers.*]

FRANCIS: Cold? You shouldn't be, it's warm.

[*He takes off his jacket and puts it over her shoulders. They dance, contented and happy. She nuzzles into him.* STEF *crawls onto the table. He steals a spoon and puts it in his jacket. Sitting on the table, he rocks back and forth, ecstatically happy.*]

ACT TWO

SCENE ONE

The living room of a working-class house, morning. A coffin lies on a table surrounded by flowers. FRANCIS *stands before it.* MRS WITCOMBE, *a neighbour, enters.*

MRS WITCOMBE: They'll be in in a moment.

FRANCIS: And what happens then?

MRS WITCOMBE: We follow them to the cemetery.
   [*Pause.*]
   So it'll be only us and her mates from work?
   [FRANCIS *nods.*]
   No relatives?

FRANCIS: I think she had relations in the country — in New South Wales, I think — but they didn't get on. Once Dad remarried, I was the only person she had.

MRS WITCOMBE: Your mum was always quiet. Kept to herself. Lived next door for twenty-odd years and ... When I die, it'll be the same. Some distant cousins in Perth, very distant cousins in England ... but, of course, we don't keep in touch. [*Looking at the corpse*] Never seen this dress before; it's gorgeous.

FRANCIS: Her honeymoon dress.

MRS WITCOMBE: Looking so calm.
   [*Pause.*]
   At least it was quick.
   [PETER *enters.* MRS WITCOMBE *doesn't notice him.*]
   She was very proud of you. 'My son the engineer!' Such rotten luck. When I was young and I saw a car for the first time — I was a country girl like your mother — I was as frightened of it as my horse was. I had every right to be. She gripped my hand so tightly as we waited for the ambulance to come ... see, it's still bruised. I'll see what's happening outside.
   [*She exits. Silence.*]

PETER: Lots of flowers; she must have been well liked.

FRANCIS: Her workmates. She worked in the same shoe factory for years and all her boss could give her was a brand new pair of shoes. In our neighbourhood flowers mean death. Mum said she had only ever saved money for herself twice: the first time for her trousseau, the second for her funeral, so she could go off 'like a real swell'.

[*Silence.*]

PETER: Do you still want to return to Hobart with me tomorrow?

[FRANCIS *nods.*]

But what about the house and things?

FRANCIS: It was rented. The landlord wants it cleaned up and empty by Tuesday. I told Mrs Witcombe that if she cleaned it up she could have anything she wanted.

PETER: But don't you want to keep a few mementos? You can't cut loose entirely.

FRANCIS: I've got a few photographs; that's all I want. [*Looking around the room*] What a life, eh? Struggle hard, marry a bastard, struggle hard, have an ungrateful son, earn enough to live in a dump. Second-hand furniture, concrete backyard and on the walls Saint Teresa and facing her a picture of the nineteen thirty Collingwood football team. If Collingwood won we had fish and chips; if they lost we didn't eat. [*Moving over to it*] Signed by all of them: Collier, Coventry ... She plucked up all her courage to go down to training one night and got all of the team to sign it. I was with her, crimson with embarrassment. She was so happy you would have thought she had had an audience with the Pope.

PETER: Why don't you take it with you?

FRANCIS: Mrs Witcombe's daughter has had her eye on it for years. Mum promised it to her.

PETER: You'll regret it if you don't take a few things to remind you.

FRANCIS: One should forget the past. Do you know why I never invited you here?

[PETER *shakes his head.*]

Because I was too ashamed.

46

SCENE TWO

A room in the asylum, evening. MAC *sits at a table.* WILLIAM *watches him. There is a manual skills test on the table. A recording of* AYRE'S *voice plays.* MAC *doesn't really listen to it.* AYRE'S *voice is slow and deliberate, as if trying to make herself understood.*

AYRE'S VOICE: Past riverrun 'n' turn o' kelp int' muddy moss, seay green 'n' here. There! Ghost 'n' sprit time. Goldy lifey, glommen lifey. Thee dreamytime in greeny belch o' 'eaven. Sprits o' cunty dell. Circle o' greeny 'ome! Nowt 'ome. Burst mouth, hairy brain 'n' cradlepain. Pitch dark glommen is dry sheb and rottin' tarse. The circle is burst ...

WILLIAM: Are you listening? That is Ayre's voice. There is nothing wrong with your vocal cords and yet you don't speak. Try again.

   [WILLIAM *makes elementary sounds.*]

Copy me.

   [*But* MAC *isn't interested.* WILLIAM *turns off the gramophone.*]

All right, let's get back to the test, then. Now concentrate this time, Mac. Concentrate!

   [MAC *is exhausted. He angrily throws the manual skills test on the ground.*]

[*Angrily*] Pick it up!

   [MAC, *obedient as a child, does so.* WILLIAM, *annoyed at his own anger, stoops to help him, then sits back on the chair.*]

I know it's late. But concentrate, please. I'm just as tired as you are. [*Smiling*] I'm going to conquer you. Understand you. Now let's go through this again. We'll get it right this time.

   [*Silence.* MAC *makes no move on the manual skills test.*]

If you do it right you can go back to your ward and see Angel. Angel. Do that test and you can go and see Angel.

   [MAC *starts on his test.*]

SCENE THREE

The asylum gardens, afternoon. The wind sounds through the trees. MAC *sits on a distant bench wearing an asylum uniform.* STEF *imitates the wind. His asylum jacket is very dirty.* BETSHEB *stands downstage in her beautiful bright dress. At her feet is a magazine. A magpie sings; she imitates its call. She begins to sing much more comprehensibly than before.*

BETSHEB: [singing]

> Glow white in 'er dress,
> Gold, gold in 'er hair.
> Ruby are 'er lips,
> Love, love is e'rywhere.

[*The bird sings again.* BETSHEB *lies on her back and spreads out the dress like a fan. She strokes her dress: the material feels wonderful — so does the grass: warm and cosy. She feels her breasts and stomach: like a child unaware of anyone else she enjoys the sensations of her own body. A woman,* DR SIMON, *enters.*]

DR SIMON: [*to* BETSHEB] Such a dress! I would kill for one like that. Happy?

BETSHEB: Yes.

DR SIMON: [*picking up a magazine*] Who wouldn't be on a day like this? Been looking at the pictures? Which ones do you like best? Aeroplanes? The cricketers? That's Don Bradman. The dancers? The weddings?

[BETSHEB *laughs at a private joke. She knows which pictures she likes best but she is not going to tell* DR SIMON.]

You're not going to tell me?

[*As* BETSHEB *continues to laugh,* DR SIMON *goes to* MAC.]

Mac, don't be so down-in-the-dumps. Come on, the man is waiting. You'll like him. He'll take your photograph. Do you want your photograph taken?

[FRANCIS *enters in army uniform with a bunch of*

flowers. He watches DR SIMON *trying to coax* MAC.]
I thought you liked seeing pictures of yourself. Come
on, for me. Come on, Mac, it won't take long.
[*She leads him off.* FRANCIS *approaches* BETSHEB, *who
still laughs to herself.*]
FRANCIS: What's so funny?
BETSHEB: Thou!
[*He gives her the flowers. She smells them deeply. He sits
down next to her and they kiss gently.*]
FRANCIS: [*indicating the dress*] Beautiful. The nurses
wanted it but I said it was for you. Only you. Elizabeth
helped me find it.
[*Pause.*]
Why is Mac being photographed?
[BETSHEB *takes no notice of the question as she feels*
FRANCIS' *uniform.*]
He's jealous of us, you know.
BETSHEB: Peter?
FRANCIS: He should have reached England by now. He'll
be stationed there. Live there.
[*Pause.*]
The nurse said you and the others visited Angel's
grave yesterday.
BETSHEB: Flowers, like this.
[*She bends down and puts her ear to the ground.*]
I ear op'n t' the Angel sprit.
FRANCIS: I spoke to Ayre before coming out here; she's
looking better.
BETSHEB: She mus' live. She mus'! She say t' me: 'I mus'
live!' [*Waving at the distance*] 'Ello!
FRANCIS: Who's that?
BETSHEB: Lorry. Gard-aner.
FRANCIS: The gardener?
BETSHEB: I 'elp 'im.
FRANCIS: I hope you won't help him in that dress.
BETSHEB: This dress? Nowt dirt. Me weddon dress.
FRANCIS: It's your good dress. Your best dress. You
know we are not allowed. When the war is over you'll
leave this place.

BETSHEB: Wid Ayre 'n' Stef 'n' Mac?

FRANCIS: [*amused*] Yes. Ayre, Stef, Mac and you.

[BETSHEB *is suddenly disturbed. She jumps up and motions to a distant building.*]

BETSHEB: There. Our bedibyes. Glommen time.

FRANCIS: You go to bed at night?

BETSHEB: There. Glommen time. There is a man, he listens, speakin' t' glommen demon. This girl ...

[*She squeezes her head like a vice.*]

She bits 'er arm.

[*She demonstrates a girl biting her own arm in an obsessional, horrific way.*]

I 'ate glommen time 'ere. 'Eads burst, outburstin' wid demons.

FRANCIS: [*soothingly*] William can't get you out of that ward; the asylum's too crowded. Those people are mad, not you. The Government says you've got to stay here. You know that.

BETSHEB: Me quim is burnin'.

[*She touches* FRANCIS' *genitals.*]

FRANCIS: Betsheb!

BETSHEB: [*moving to him again*] Thou burning. Eyebright.

[*She jumps him again and he ducks out of the way. She chases after him. They both laugh, like children in a game.*]

FRANCIS: Not out here. Everyone's watching!

BETSHEB: Francis! Francis! Francis!

FRANCIS: I'll turn the hose on you.

BETSHEB: [*laughing*] Burnin'. Burnin'.

[*She grabs him. He falls to the ground. She kisses him.*]

FRANCIS: [*pushing her away slightly*] Betsheb, I have to tell you something.

[*She grabs him and smothers his face with quick kisses. He pushes her away, annoyed.*]

This is serious!

[BETSHEB *doesn't notice his annoyance.*]

BETSHEB: The belle she spoonin' the gent. 'E whoopin'.

[*She grabs him again.*]

FRANCIS: [*angrily*] No!
[*Almost immediately he is annoyed with himself for getting angry. She looks hurt and confused.*]
Listen. [*Touching his uniform*] You remember what I told you this uniform meant? I am in the army. Australia is at war with Germany and Italy. We have to fight to protect ourselves. To protect you, to save you from hurt, our families from hurt.
VOICE: [*off*] Mr Morris, the taxi's here!
FRANCIS: [*calling*] Tell him I won't be a moment. [*To* BETSHEB] I joined up to fight because we have to. And now I know I must fight for you, for Stef. The Germans are demons. Do you understand any of this?
[*She nods, but it's clear she doesn't.*]
I'm being shipped out tomorrow. Europe. Remember the map of the world we looked at? Well, I'm going to Europe. I won't be seeing you for some time. Goodbye.
BETSHEB: [*shocked*] 'Goodbye'?
FRANCIS: But not for long. I knew a couple of days ago but couldn't tell you. Too much of a coward. This dress is my going-away present for you. And this.
[*He gives her a wrist watch.*]
You can watch the hands move, learn to tell the time. You wind it, make it go like this.
[BETSHEB *is still shocked and pays little attention.*]
BETSHEB: 'Goodbye'?
[*The taxi horn beeps.*]
FRANCIS: I must go. I'll write letter. William said he'd read them to you.
BETSHEB: Nowt 'Goodbye'.
FRANCIS: I have to; it's my duty.
BETSHEB: Nowt 'Goodbye'!
[*He kisses her.*]
FRANCIS: This hurts me too. I love you ... do you understand?
BETSHEB: Nowt 'Goodbye'.
[*He begins to go, then stops briefly to pat* STEF *on the head.*]

FRANCIS: Goodbye, Stef.

> [STEF *laughs and rolls over and over.* FRANCIS *pauses to look back at* BETSHEB. *She looks at him, confused and hurt. The taxi horn beeps again: he must go. He exits.*]

BETSHEB: [*quietly*] Nowt 'Goodbye'. [*Crying out, throwing away the watch*] Nowt 'Goodbye'!

SCENE FOUR

The asylum gardens, early evening. WILLIAM, *in dinner jacket, sits on the bench upstage. He watches* STEF, MAC, AYRE *and* BETSHEB *downstage. All of the group wear asylum clothes.* MAC *sleeps curled up.* STEF *examines his shoe by himself.* BETSHEB *half cradles* AYRE, *chewing bits of bread and, like a sparrow feeding its young, passing the chewed bread into* AYRE'*s mouth.* AYRE *is fading, but she is desperate to live long enough to pass on their language and memories to* BETSHEB. *It is difficult for* AYRE *to get the words out.*

AYRE: Demon 'ollarin' in glommen time.

BETSHEB: 'Demon 'ollarin' in glommen time.'

> [*Silence.*]

AYRE: Sprits o' rack 'n' cat, doomtime.'

BETSHEB: 'Sprits o' rack 'n' cat, doomtime.'

> [*Silence.* ELIZABETH, *wearing an expensive evening gown, enters and watches, unnoticed.*]

AYRE: Sprits adorate quim sold for sinbread.

BETSHEB: 'Sprits adorate quim sold for sinbread.'

AYRE: Albion is glommentime, rack 'n' cat time.

BETSHEB: 'Albion is glommentime, rack 'n' cat time.'

> [*Silence.* BETSHEB *feeds* AYRE. ELIZABETH *goes towards* WILLIAM.]

ELIZABETH: The driver is waiting.

> [*He looks up, puzzled.*]

You said we should pick you up on the way to Government House.

WILLIAM: I wanted to see if Ayre was all right.

ELIZABETH: You're always here. Why isn't Ayre inside? She looks very ill.

WILLIAM: She has a great fear of dying in her room. They'll go in soon for dinner.

ELIZABETH: I'm curious, William: what do you do when you come to visit them?

WILLIAM: Nothing much. Check their health. Watch.

ELIZABETH: You're forever here. The hospital's always ringing me. 'Where's Doctor Archer?' 'He's gone to stare at the madmen', I say.

WILLIAM: They're not mad.

ELIZABETH: They just do a very good impersonation of it.

[Pause.]

WILLIAM: Ayre is teaching Betsheb — not teaching, passing on their culture, her memories.

ELIZABETH: Do you read Francis's letters to her?

WILLIAM: Each one I have to read dozens of times. She misses him terribly.

AYRE: [to BETSHEB] Glommen sprits o' cut-throat kin.

BETSHEB: 'Glommen sprits o' cut-throat kin.'

AYRE: Pass 'elly gate t' goldy dell.

BETSHEB: 'Pass 'elly gate t' goldy dell.'

ELIZABETH: [to WILLIAM] What a pathetic group they look, like those Aboriginals in shanty towns.

WILLIAM: She's teaching Betsheb about the night-time spirits.

ELIZABETH: Come on, the Governor is waiting.

[He stands.]

Your bow tie.

[An envelope falls from his lap. As he straightens his bow tie, ELIZABETH picks up the envelope.]

What's in here?

WILLIAM: The editor of the Medical Journal was going to publish them.

ELIZABETH: [handing him the envelope] What are they?

WILLIAM: The Chief Psychiatrist here decided she wanted photographs of Mac's interesting medical condition. [Handing the photographs to ELIZABETH] He was always ashamed of his deformity and so that's what they photographed in brilliant close-ups. The reason why Ayre and the rest are here is because Mac couldn't have children. He knows that. And look what they go and do.

ELIZABETH: You would have been as callous as that.

WILLIAM: Once.

ELIZABETH: Your tie. [*Straightening his tie*] You smell like a brewery.

WILLIAM: I drink to forget what we've done to them.

ELIZABETH: There was nothing you could do.

AYRE: [*to* BETSHEB] Pearly dawn pass glommen time, thou pass demon time. Pass tempest 'n' temper time.

WILLIAM: [*to* ELIZABETH] It would have been nice for that to have been the Australian language.

ELIZABETH: When you've been drinking I can never tell when you're serious or not.

WILLIAM: Their culture is more authentic than ours. We Australians have assumed the garb of a hand-me-down culture, but at our heart is a desert. For their appalling ignorance and pathetic beliefs they at least have a real core, an essence.

ELIZABETH: When you're in your cups you have a disturbing tendency to philosophise. I know this mood of yours: no sarcastic remarks about Singapore at the dinner.

WILLIAM: Why shouldn't I? The pompous ass said only a month ago that Singapore was impregnable. Thousands of Australians are in prison camps because of British stupidity. Betsheb.

[BETSHEB *turns to him. He motions at the sky.*]

Tempest time.

[BETSHEB *looks up at the sky.*]

Probably tonight.

BETSHEB: [*smiling*] Yes.

WILLIAM: You'd better get Ayre in. 'Bye, Ayre. Mac. 'Bye, Betsheb. I'll see you tomorrow.

[MAC *picks up* AYRE *and carries her inside.*]

She won't allow the nurses to touch her.

ELIZABETH: She's not long for this world.

WILLIAM: Probably not.

ELIZABETH: [*sarcastically*] But you've still got her voice
on record. Don't be a hypocrite. You're glad that
they've been hidden away; you've had them all to
yourself. If you don't recognise that, then you're
blind. We had better hurry, the Governor doesn't like
to be kept waiting.

    [*They exit.*]

SCENE FIVE

On one side of the stage FRANCIS, *in army uniform with
greatcoat covering his shoulders, writes by lamplight. On the
other is the asylum gardens, night.* BETSHEB *washes a naked*
STEF *with a bucket and sponge.*

FRANCIS: My darling Betsheb, tomorrow morning I go
into battle for the first time. The German planes have
been pounding us since we arrived.

    [BETSHEB *washes* STEF's *body as he makes wind noises.
Both seem very happy.* WILLIAM *enters and, unnoticed,
watches the pair.*]

Crete is desolate and rocky. Why should we defend
this country? We are fighting over a place as desolate
as the moon.

    [BETSHEB *washes* STEF's *face. He laughs and then rolls
away. She catches him and continues to wash his face.*]

When we arrived we ran into a local priest who had lost
both his legs. He felt sorry for us and said: 'This is a bad
world and you have lost your way in it.' It was easy to
see what he meant. The paddocks were covered in
burning tanks and dying men. I imagine a battle is like
being caught in a butcher shop that is burning down.

    [BETSHEB *washes* STEF's *groin.*]

BETSHEB: [*softly, singing*]

> Hey, hey,
> The girlie say,
> Rub a dub, dub,
> Spoonin' in the hay.

FRANCIS: It is said that if we win here, then we'll stop the Germans and the war will end. There will be a peace. But will I be alive to see it?
[BETSHEB *tickles* STEF's *feet. He laughs wildly, she joins in. Their laughter is joyous.*]
Betsheb, I am scared. I do not want to die.

SCENE SIX

The asylum gardens, dusk. BETSHEB *stands on* MAC's *shoulders. They turn slowly, her face to the darkening sky. As if in a dream,* ANGEL's *penny whistle sounds.*

BETSHEB: [*singing*]

> Rain, rain, go thy way,
> Come a-back ne'er a day.

[*As* BETSHEB *repeats the song, unconsciously she strokes* MAC's *face sensuously. He is pleased to be touched by* BETSHEB.]
[*Softly*] Francis ...
[MAC *breaks away. Astonished,* BETSHEB *tumbles to the ground.* MAC *heads off.* BETSHEB, *perplexed by his behaviour, chases after him. He throws her off and exits angrily.*]

SCENE SEVEN

The asylum gardens, late at night. Rain and hail pour down. A cry of pain comes from the distance. Dimly, a figure hurries out into the garden. It is DR SIMON, *carrying an umbrella and a flashlight. The beam darts here and there.*

DR SIMON: Betsheb! Are you out here?
  [*Pause.*]
 Betsheb. Bring Ayre inside.
  [*Pause.*]
 Betsheb! Answer me! Where are you? Come out of the rain.
  [*She exits towards C Ward. Silence. Thunder.* BETSHEB *drags* AYRE *into the rain.*]
BETSHEB: [*crying*] Thou mus' nowt die. Thou mus' live!
  [*She stops to catch her breath.*]
 Goldy green breathen int' thee, rain breathen int' thee.
  [*She rolls* AYRE *back and forth.* AYRE *moans in agony.*]
 The earth breathen int' thee. Thou mus' live!
  [DR SIMON *enters again, at a distance.*]
DR SIMON: [*off*] Betsheb! Betsheb! Where are you?
  [BETSHEB *huddles over* AYRE'*s body. Pause.* DR SIMON *retreats. Once sure she has gone,* BETSHEB *turns her attention back to* AYRE. *She is barely breathing.*]
BETSHEB: [*breathing into* AYRE'*s mouth*] I am in thee, thee in me. [*Thumping* AYRE] Breathen! Breathen the tempest! Breathen the rain! [*Crying out, desperately*] Breathen the world! Thee must breathen the world!
  [*But* AYRE *is dead.*]
 Nowt die! Nowt die!
  [*She wails in fear and horror.*]
 Breathen! Breathen the world! The world is breathen thee! Mumma! Breathen!

SCENE EIGHT

The asylum gardens, a pleasant Autumn day. MAC *lies on the ground, dead. A bloodied knife lies next to him.* DR SIMON *enters with a camera. She turns* MAC *over: his crotch is bloodied. He has castrated himself.* DR SIMON *sees someone in the distance.*

DR SIMON: Get back to your ward, Richard.
　　[*She watches Richard go.*]
　　Hurry up.
　　[*She turns her attention to the corpse and, taking careful aim, takes a photograph. She doesn't like the way the body is arranged, so she shifts it slightly with her foot and takes a closer picture. Silence. She stares at the corpse.*]
　　[*Quietly*] It's over now; you are released.

SCENE NINE

The asylum gardens, a winter's day. WILLIAM *sits on the bench wearing a coat.* STEF *and* BETSHEB *sit on the grass wearing hand-me-down coats over their asylum uniforms.* BETSHEB *massages* STEF'*s scalp.* WILLIAM *reads a letter to her.*

WILLIAM: 'Some people say the war will be over by Christmas, others say it will go on forever. There is no point to this slaughter. The Germans will lose, but they don't give in; they would sooner destroy the world than surrender. My handwriting is bad. We are snowed in and my hands are shaking with the cold. The snow and the blood are endless.'
　　[WILLIAM *points.*]
　　Like the snow on Mount Wellington.
　　[BETSHEB *nods.*]
BETSHEB: Pass snow; nowt more outcastin'.

WILLIAM: Once the snow thaws, perhaps his exile will be over. Nowt more outcastin'. [*Continuing the letter*] 'I want to write about more pleasant things, Betsheb, but the war is my world at the moment. But once it is over I will return. Goodbye for now, my love, Francis.'

> [STEF *no longer wants his head massaged. He moves away and coughs deeply. He laughs.* BETSHEB *rises and takes the letter from* WILLIAM.]

You must have quite a collection now.

> [*She puts it down the front of her dress. There is a blast of icy wind.* WILLIAM *shivers.*]

What a wind, eh? Straight from the South Pole.

> [BETSHEB *ponders. Silence.* DR SIMON *enters and stands at a distance, watching the odd trio.*]

BETSHEB: Nurse Greene got child.

WILLIAM: A baby boy.

BETSHEB: The belly o' 'er quim. Lovely.

WILLIAM: She and her husband had been trying for years to have a child.

BETSHEB: Francis outcastin'; come back 'n' look at 'is belle 'n' 'e think 'the dead moon o' me cunt.'

WILLIAM: We don't know for certain.

BETSHEB: Me bod shakin' like a leaf, out o' the blue.

WILLIAM: Those fits you have are rare.

BETSHEB: Me bod in the toothy bite o' a bad dream.

> [*Silence.*]

DR SIMON: What is Betsheb talking about?

WILLIAM: Nothing important.

DR SIMON: I'm curious.

WILLIAM: She just talks about things that interest her.

DR SIMON: And they don't interest you?

WILLIAM: Of course they do.

DR SIMON: Then why wouldn't I be interested?

> [*Pause.* WILLIAM *turns his attention back to* BETSHEB.]

WILLIAM: [*to* BETSHEB] Don't be afraid of your body —

DR SIMON: [*interrupting*] If I knew the language or if you translated for me, then I would be able to help them.

WILLIAM: Like you helped Mac with the photographs?

DR SIMON: I am Chief Psychiatrist here. I have every right to have patients photographed: photographs are a legitimate record of a patient's condition.

WILLIAM: You treated him as if he were a freak.

DR SIMON: That's not true. You have turned them against everyone except yourself. I have been here over four years and I still can't understand her.

WILLIAM: [*coldly*] Perhaps you're stupid.

DR SIMON: [*angrily*] You come here drunk. You've been relieved of your own post. Remember, you are only a visitor. You have no authority here.

[STEF *coughs.*]

If you really cared for him you wouldn't let him lie out in the cold. He should be brought inside.

[*She takes a step towards* STEF. BETSHEB *moves in front of him.*]

WILLIAM: If you touch him, Betsheb will kill you.

[DR SIMON *stops.*]

[*Smiling*] Perhaps you had best get out of the cold, Doctor Simon.

DR SIMON: One day, Doctor Archer, you'll realise what you've done to them.

WILLIAM: I know what I've done: I've protected them from the likes of you.

[DR SIMON *returns inside.* BETSHEB *sits down on the wet grass and looks at the watch* FRANCIS *gave her.*]

BETSHEB: Time is slow.

[*She looks at her watch, willing time to go faster.* STEF *lies prone on the ground, silent.* WILLIAM *puts up his collar to shield himself from the cold wind. Silence.*]

SCENE TEN

The asylum gardens, night. There is a moon. BETSHEB *sits on the bench staring at the night sky.*

BETSHEB: 'I cup me ear t' the glommen bird. Soul o' the

dead. Cryin out "Donna burst yer 'eart, the bird is me."'

[*Faint sounds of a party and dance songs of the forties come from the distance. A man in his thirties enters wearing a party hat or mask.*]

JAMES: How you going? I was over there watching you talking to yourself. The New Year's party is pretty good, eh?

[BETSHEB *is nervous.*]

You've seen me around, haven't you? James, remember? I've been here almost as long as you. The nurses call me 'Jimmy'; me mum, 'Jim'. I saw you crawling out the window. I see you do that most nights. I can talk to you tonight because the ward assistant is drunk. He's not bad, Bert; keeps us up with the war news. I wanted to fight. I tried to join up. I said, 'I want to murder Germans.' They refused me. They said they didn't want murderers in their army. I should have said I wanted to kill Germans. James, Jim, Jimmy, murder, kill ... No wonder I'm at a loss in the outside world; I haven't got me language skills right. Want a fuck?

[*She doesn't understand.*]

I can't make it plainer than that. I suppose I should ask you with words tied up with little blue bow ties but I don't know any.

[*He comes closer. She stiffens.*]

You can call me 'James', 'Jim', 'Jimmy'; I'll answer to them all.

[*He makes a grab at her; she ducks away.*]

[*Annoyed*] Why the problem? You're as fuckin' mad as me; why put up a front?

BETSHEB: [*quietly, explaining*] Francis. Francis, 'e outcastin'.

JAMES: No wonder none of us can understand you: it sounds like a mouthful of marbles.

[*He lunges and grabs at her. She stands still, scared.*]

Others are scared of you, think you're some kind of witch. Not me. I see you pissing out here, rubbing

yourself and I know. Look at you, like a bird in a trap.
  [*He slowly pulls her closer.*]
I have dreamed of fuckin' you; now I'll make it real.
DR SIMON: [*off, quietly*] Jimmy.
  [*Pause.*]
Jimmy, let her go.
  [JAMES *lets her go.*]
JAMES: [*looking off*] Hello, Doctor Simon.
DR SIMON: Go back to the party.
JAMES: Why pick on me? She's always out, every night,
  yapping to herself.
DR SIMON: Back to your ward.
  [JAMES *goes. Silence.* BETSHEB *lifts up her dress,
  offering her body in gratitude to* DR SIMON.]
Put down your dress, Betsheb, and go to bed. Stef
needs you; he's very sick.

SCENE ELEVEN

The asylum gardens, a spring day. Birds are singing.
BETSHEB *drags out the body of* STEF. *He is dead, but she tries
to play with him as she once did.* DR SIMON *enters.*

DR SIMON: Let him go, Betsheb. Come on, let him go …
  He has to be examined by the coroner.
  [*She advances on* BETSHEB, *who growls like an animal
  and lashes out.*]
Little bitch.
  [BETSHEB *growls softly.*]
Like a bloody animal.
  [*Pause.*]
[*Angrily*] He's dead. If you hadn't let him lie on the wet
grass he wouldn't be.
  [WILLIAM *enters. His clothes are dirty and he is very
  drunk.*]
WILLIAM: [*to* DR SIMON, *smiling*] Fell into the flower bed.
  Blood and bone. Boy, do I pong! Betsheb!
DR SIMON: Doctor Archer, she won't let go of Stef.

WILLIAM: So what?

DR SIMON: He's been dead since early this morning.

[WILLIAM *is shocked for a moment.*]

WILLIAM: Stef?

BETSHEB: [*anguished*] Stef: 'e dead!

WILLIAM: No, not possible.

DR SIMON: The coroner's waiting; we have to get Stef away from her.

[WILLIAM*'s sense of duty as a doctor returns.*]

WILLIAM: Yes, yes. [*To* BETSHEB] You must let him go, Betsheb, there is nothing you can do. Nothing more.

BETSHEB: 'e me las' blood. Stef is me las' blood. I am cast t' the windy. 'e me las' blood, boyo.

WILLIAM: I know, but you must give him up.

[BETSHEB *cradles* STEF, *focusing all her attention on him.* WILLIAM *starts to walk towards her, but trips and falls. He lands and turns on his back, grinning broadly.*] Whoops-a-daisy.

[*For a moment he is bewildered, then he realises where he is.*]

[*To* BETSHEB] I'm sorry.

DR SIMON: You're putrid drunk, Doctor Archer!

WILLIAM: God, help me, some women are observant. Yes, Doctor, I am going putrescent with alcohol.

DR SIMON: You're as crazy as she is.

WILLIAM: I'm just drunk. Get a whiff of my clothes!

[*He laughs.* DR SIMON *hurries off.*]

[*Calling after her*] Call the cops! [*Yelling*] Call anyone you bloody-well please!

[*Silence. He stares at* BETSHEB *for some time, at a loss. All her attention remains on* STEF *as she cradles him. Pause.*

[*Brushing her hair*] How I wanted to study you. To find out. I thought if I did discover everything, then I'd know. You know, of course, that this drunken old man loves you just as much as Francis does. Don't wait for him, he hasn't written in a year, he's free of you. Run away, head for the hills. Nowt more outcastin'.

[*Silence.*]

I shouldn't have let you destroy me.

BETSHEB: [*looking at* WILLIAM, *quietly, almost beyond pain*]
Stef ... 'E dead.

SCENE TWELVE

The ruins of Berlin, evening, 1945. FRANCIS, *now a
lieutenant, enters carrying a pistol. He is dirty, worn and
wearing a heavy army coat. He stops and looks around.*
PRIVATE CORRIS *enters, also rugged up, carrying a rifle.
Nearby on the ground are the remains of a huge statue: the
head of Frederick the Great, its face riddled with bullet holes.*

CORRIS: I'm pretty sure I saw the bugger head this way.
FRANCIS: He's probably gone through those ruins there.
CORRIS: He wouldn't get far: there's the Americans on
the other side.
[*Silence.*]
Sorry I fucked it up. When I turned me back he was off
like a flash.
FRANCIS: [*shrugging*] It'll soon be too dark to see
anything.
CORRIS: Yeah, the fires are starting up. The homeless.
What a fuckin' mess, eh? They'll have to rebuild Berlin
from scratch. They live like rats in a tip. [*Looking at the
head*] Not much bird shit.
FRANCIS: They deserved it: they started it; they were so
bloody proud of their thousand-year Reich.
CORRIS: [*examining a hole in the head*] Jesus, Doctor, I've
got a splitting headache.
[*He laughs.*]
I once saw Mo at the Tiv; me girlfriend said I was
funnier. Who do you reckon it is?
[FRANCIS *shakes his head.*]
It's not Hitler. Some old king, I guess. Wonder where
the rest of him is. [*Looking around*] A leg there ...
there's some angels. [*Sitting on the head*] Have to be
careful I don't get a nose up me bum. You know what

I heard yesterday? After they strung up Mussolini and his mistress they pissed and shat on them. Bet you the same people who were saluting him the day before did it. Will we keep going or what?

FRANCIS: No point. Be too dark to see soon. He'll hide in the ruins somewhere, find some old mate, change his identity ... Doesn't matter.

CORRIS: Maybe the Yanks will get him.

FRANCIS: So what? You saw them with those scientists the other day putting them on the plane. Like they were kings. Going to America to get well-paid jobs and yet they created the planes, the bombs, the rockets —

CORRIS: [*interrupting*] This fella was no scientist.

FRANCIS: He was Goebbels' right-hand man. He'll probably end up like the scientists: get off scot free, probably find himself running a huge American publicity firm.

CORRIS: Maybe they'll go to trial.

FRANCIS: They are war criminals: who needs a trial? We should execute them straight away.

CORRIS: Got a real bee in your bonnet.

FRANCIS: [*coldly*] And you're a bloody idiot: you let him go.

[*Silence.*]

[*Looking around*] This is where the world ended.

CORRIS: What I wouldn't give to be back in Australia. Know what I learned in four years of fighting the Krauts? One German phrase: 'I surrender.' And to prove I was Australian I'd hop about like this.

[*He starts to hop. Suddenly* FRANCIS *pulls out his revolver and fires at* CORRIS. CORRIS *ducks. There is a cry from the ruins. A figure wearing a dirty suit jumps into view and runs for* CORRIS' *gun.*]

FRANCIS: Get out of the way, Corris.

[*He fires and hits the* MAN *again.*]

Grab him.

[CORRIS *and the* MAN *struggle with the rifle, but the* MAN *is weak and bleeding badly. He falls to the ground.*]

[*To the* MAN, *pointing his revolver*] Don't move.

CORRIS: That's the bugger, Lieutenant. [*Looking closely*]
  Jeez, he's badly hit.
FRANCIS: He must have been waiting all the time, waiting
  to jump you and get your rifle.
CORRIS: [*motioning with his rifle*] On your feet, Fritz. [*To
  FRANCIS*] I think he's hurt too bad. One in the leg isn't
  too bad, but the chest ...
FRANCIS: Understand English?
MAN: English? *Nein.*
FRANCIS: Get someone to help us carry him back.
CORRIS: Those Americans will help us. Be back in ten.
  [CORRIS *heads off. Silence.*]
FRANCIS: Not such a big boy now. What's the point?
  You'll get off.
  [*The* MAN *is dying.*]
MAN: Kill me.
  [FRANCIS *is surprised.*]
  Kill me. Please.
  [*The* MAN *is in incredible pain.* FRANCIS *puts his gun
  to the* MAN'*s head and calmly shoots him.*]

SCENE THIRTEEN

WILLIAM'*s study, night.* WILLIAM *sits in a high-backed chair
finishing the remains of a bottle of whiskey. He is drunk, but
full of purpose. On his lap is an open cut-throat razor. He
listens to a recording of* AYRE'*s voice for the umpteenth time.
As she slowly speaks he unconsciously translates.*

AYRE'S VOICE: Past riverrun 'n' turn o' kelp int' muddy
  moss, seay green 'n' here. There! Ghost 'n' sprit time.
  Goldy lifey, glommen lifey. Thee dreamytime in
  greeny belch o' 'eaven. Sprits o' cunty dell. Circle o'
  greeny 'ome! Nowt 'ome. Burst mouth, 'airy brain 'n'
  cradlepain. Pitch dark glommen is dry sheb and rottin'
  tarse. The circle is burst ...
WILLIAM: 'We came past river, past tides of kelp and

mud, moss and into the sea of green and came to here. There! The time of our ancestors. A dreamtime in the green stomach of heaven. All around the spirits of the fertile valley. Home. It is not home. Then something happened: there were hair lips, soft brains and children in pain. A darkness of sterile girls and boys. The circle is burst. Broken.'

[*The sound of burning wood is heard faintly. Something is burning close to* WILLIAM, *but he does not hear it, or doesn't care.*]

AYRE'S VOICE: 'Ear us, William, William. Keep us in that box. We is talkin' t' thee. T' thee. The circle is burst. I ne'er more cup me ear to the glommen bird. I ne'er more helter-skelterin' wid the glommen sprits; foe 'n' friend.

WILLIAM: 'Hear us, William. Keep us in that box. We are talking to you. To *you!* The circle is broken. I'll never more listen to the night-birds. Never more dance with the night spirits, the good and the bad.'

[WILLIAM *finishes his drink and puts down the empty glass.*]

ELIZABETH: [*off, banging on the door, yelling*] Bill! William! Are you in there?

AYRE'S VOICE: Listen t' us, William, 'ear us words, 'member us, 'elp us, us who is born in card, cradlepain. Nowt more outcastin'.

WILLIAM: 'Listen to us, William. Hear our words. Remember us. Help us, who were born in pain. No more exile.'

ELIZABETH: William, answer me!

AYRE'S VOICE: Nowt more outcastin'.

WILLIAM: 'No more exile.'

[WILLIAM *does not hear* ELIZABETH. *He picks up the razor and calmly slits his throat. The fire grows loud.*]

SCENE FOURTEEN

The asylum gardens, late afternoon. BETSHEB *sits on the bench. Some flowers, pulled up by the roots, are scattered around her. Around her mouth are traces of dried blood. She wears a white hospital gown which is stained with urine and menstrual blood. She has lost control of herself.* DR SIMON *enters, surprised by* BETSHEB's *appearance.*

DR SIMON: What has happened, Betsheb?
> [BETSHEB *doesn't answer.*]

Larry said someone tore up all his flower beds: it was you, wasn't it?
> [*Pause.*]

You must look after yourself. Come inside, let's clean you up.
> [DR SIMON *grabs her. Suddenly* BETSHEB *lashes out and knocks the doctor down.*]

BETSHEB: Way! Way!
> [BETSHEB *looks wild.* DR SIMON *gets up and moves away.*]

DR SIMON: Come on, Betsheb, come inside.

BETSHEB: [*screaming*] Nowt more!

DR SIMON: If you don't calm down I'll have to get the ward assistants to help me.

BETSHEB: [*screaming*] Nowt more!
> [DR SIMON *hurries off for help.* BETSHEB *looks wildly about her.*]

[*Screaming*] Nowt more! [*Looking up at the sky*] Nowt more!
> [*Suddenly there is thunder. It is as if she cries out for the destruction of the world. The more she screams at the heavens, the louder the thunder and lightening grows.*]

SCENE FIFTEEN

A prison courtyard, Berlin, afternoon. FRANCIS *sits on the ground against a wall and soaks up the last rays of sun. Silence.*

AMERICAN VOICE: [*off, crying out*] Hoy, hoy, I'm the boy! Hoy, hoy, I'm the boy!
　　[PETER *enters in a captain's uniform.* FRANCIS *doesn't notice him.* PETER *is shocked by* FRANCIS' *condition. He puts on a smile.*]
PETER: Long time no see, mate.
FRANCIS: Peter!
　　[*He stands up. They greet each other warmly.*]
　　So long, so bloody long!
PETER: Forty-two.
FRANCIS: That's right. A captain.
PETER: Didn't do so badly yourself.
　　[*There is an awkward pause.* FRANCIS *makes a sweeping, mocking gesture.*]
FRANCIS: My home.
PETER: [*trying to be light hearted*] Love the bluestone.
FRANCIS: How did you find me?
PETER: Came over from Paris a few days ago. I'm fixing up the final Australian repatriation. Heard about your case this morning. How long have you been here?
FRANCIS: Eight or nine weeks. This is my daily exercise. I'm like a lizard. I follow the sun around the courtyard, trying to warm my blood.
AMERICAN VOICE: [*off*] Hoy, hoy, I'm the boy! Hoy, hoy, I'm the boy!
FRANCIS: An American negro. Went mad and killed a whore with his bare hands 'cos she called him a nigger. [*Gesturing*] Those windows, they're black-marketeers. War criminals stare out of those windows, waiting to be sent to Nuremburg; and those windows, that's where I am: the rapists and murderers section.
AMERICAN VOICE: Hoy, hoy, I'm the boy! Hoy, hoy, I'm the boy!

FRANCIS: Actually, I'm quite at home; it reminds me of Collingwood.
> [*He walks a little to the left, looking up at the sun, closing his eyes.*]

The last bit of sun. It's freezing in the cell.

PETER: I only had time to glance at your file. The Americans think you murdered him.

FRANCIS: I did. The Kraut asked me to do it, so I obliged. Now the Australians want to show off to the Allies that they can be just as tough on their men. [*Looking at the sun*] It's going.

PETER: After years in England it was the sun I missed the most and the bright blue skies.
> [*Pause.*]

Did you know my father died?

FRANCIS: Your mum wrote to me.

PETER: Burnt to death. Most of the rear of the house was destroyed. Mother said you stopped writing to Betsheb.

FRANCIS: What could I write to her about? How could I describe what I was seeing? Civilisations perfecting death. Bombs, fighter planes, slaughtered soldiers, extermination camps, rape, blood lust. I couldn't pretend the war would end and I would return because every morning I thought I would die that day. I couldn't write any more gentle letters because I have nothing of that left inside me any more. It's gone, the little I had. Once I stopped writing to her I knew I couldn't go home again. This prison perfectly suits my state of mind; I have been bred for it, just as I have been bred to kill. Do you know that people think the war will continue only it will be between the Americans and Russians? It's as if this century has imagined a monster, concocted if from the deepest underworld of its brain and now it has escaped and is devouring everything. Nothing makes sense.

AMERICAN VOICE: Hoy, hoy, I'm the boy! Hoy, hoy, I'm the boy!

PETER: Your bitterness will pass.

FRANCIS: I can't get rid of this dream. I have built a bridge. There is a grand opening. The ribbon is cut. Bright happy people begin to walk across the bridge. It collapses like a pack of cards. I have even lost faith in my ability to build something mechanical. How I envied you with your wealth, your background, your sense of past, family, belonging. I am rootless now. It's not such a bad feeling because it's no feeling at all.

AMERICAN VOICE: Hoy, hoy, I'm the boy! [*More desperately*] Hoy, hoy, I'm the boy!

FRANCIS: I wish I could go as mad as him.

PETER: You've spent too many years fighting. Everyone has.

FRANCIS: Don't you see, Peter, the war will never stop; we humans don't give up until we perfect something. Mind made perfect matter.

PETER: It's over.

AMERICAN VOICE: [*desperately*] Hoy, hoy, I'm the boy!

   [FRANCIS *stands on tip toe to get the last rays of the sun.*]

FRANCIS: What kept me going was my memories of that time when we found them. God, I was stricken with her.

   [PETER *laughs.*]

The old geezer doing Lear; I finally realised what it was: the happy version of *King Lear.*

   [*The sun vanishes.*]

Poof! Snuffed out.

   [*Pause.*]

PETER: We were very innocent then.

FRANCIS: So were they.

AMERICAN VOICE: [*crying out*] Hoy, hoy, I'm the boy!

FRANCIS: [*calling out*] Hoy, hoy, you're the boy!

AMERICAN VOICE: [*joyfully*] Hoy, hoy, I'm the boy!

FRANCIS: Before going in I tell him that. It makes him happy. [*Holding out his hand*] I have to go in now.

PETER: You'd better. [*Smiling*] You'll have to collect your gear. You'll be flown to England tomorrow and then … a slow boat to Australia.

   [*Pause.*]

They wanted a way out of it as much as you did. No one really wants to be reminded of the war any more. Connections help, the major was a friend of my father.

[FRANCIS *is stunned.*]

AMERICAN VOICE: [*joyfully*] Hoy, hoy, I'm the boy!

PETER: The nightmare is over.

SCENE SIXTEEN

The asylum gardens, an early summer day, 1945. BETSHEB *sits, withdrawn, on the bench in a clean hospital gown. It is as if she is a doll that has had all its stuffing removed.* FRANCIS *enters in civilian clothes. He carries a large bunch of flowers. Escorting him is* DR SIMON.

DR SIMON: She always sits on that garden bench.

[*They look at her.*]

You're the first visitor she's had in a long time.

FRANCIS: No one else?

DR SIMON: No one. Not for a year.

FRANCIS: She was supposed to be released once the war was over.

DR SIMON: I know nothing about that. All files about her and her group were stolen by Doctor Archer and destroyed in his house fire. Anyway, she's not in a fit condition to be released.

[FRANCIS *takes a step towards* BETSHEB, *but* DR SIMON *speaks again.*]

It would have been better if you had never found them. They should have remained a lost tribe.

[FRANCIS *nods.*]

She was in a terrible state. Profound depressions and refusing to eat, so we had to give her electric shock treatment. Be patient with her.

[DR SIMON *exits. Silence.* FRANCIS *walks towards* BETSHEB *and stops behind her, smiling nervously.*]

FRANCIS: [*quietly*] Betsheb?

[*She doesn't hear. He walks around to face her.*]
Betsheb?
[*She doesn't seem to recognise him. He gives her the flowers: they drop from her lap onto the ground.*]
It's me. Francis. Please. Look at me.
[*She looks at him without recognition.*]
What have we done to you?
[*Silence.*]
I couldn't come back. I couldn't write any more. When the others died I didn't know what to write. I thought they were better off dead than living here.
[*Pause.*]
You're the last thing I ever wanted to hurt.
[*A long silence.*]
I didn't know this was going to happen. Perhaps I did, that's why I felt so guilty.
[*Silence.*]
Betsheb?
[*He kisses her. She doesn't respond. As he kisses her again, he takes out his revolver and points it at the side of her head.*]

SCENE SEVENTEEN

Hobart, a summer's night, 1945. The tiny Greek temple is the same as the opening scene. ELIZABETH *stands before it in Greek costume.* PETER, *in dinner jacket, plays his father's role as Orestes.*

ELIZABETH: 'You are now ready for death, yet you seem to be facing the prospect of such a hideous fate with true calm.'
PETER: 'What else should I do? I have nothing to live for.'
ELIZABETH: 'What of your family? You were once a child: who was your mother, then? Your father? Have you a sister?'
PETER: 'My sister was sacrificed for my father.'

ELIZABETH: 'I am lost too. My mother, Clytemnestra, said my brother —'

PETER: 'My darling sister! I can scarcely believe what I hear!'

[*He moves towards her. She steps away.*]

ELIZABETH: 'What are you doing? I am Head Priestess.'

PETER: 'Clytemnestra was my mother too! My father is the grandson of Pelops. Was yours?'

ELIZABETH: 'Yes.'

PETER: 'Iphigenia! We thought you were dead and now I have found you!'

ELIZABETH: 'I am happier than words can tell.'

[*They embrace.*]

'Our strange story is beyond all dreams and thought. Instead of killing you I must save you and so save us all. How I longed for my country and you, long before your coming. Orestes. How my prayer joins with yours for the renewal of our breed. We must escape.'

PETER: 'My purpose in coming here must now be revealed. I came here to steal the statue of Artemis. We shall take it back with us.'

ELIZABETH: 'You cannot do both; take the statue and leave me to die. If a man dies, a house, a name is lost, but if a woman dies it means nothing.'

PETER: 'No murderer of you shall I be. Either I escape to Argos with you or die here with you. Now I see the plan of the gods: they have intended that I should find you here. I see the strands of fate entwining themselves. Lady, I think we shall reach home!'

[MARY, *the maid, enters. Both* PETER *and* ELIZABETH *stop.*]

MARY: I'm sorry, Mrs Archer, an urgent phone call for your son.

PETER: Who is it, Mary?

MARY: The superintendent of New Norfolk Asylum, Mr Archer.

[PETER *heads off, followed by* MARY.]

ELIZABETH: [*exasperated*] Peter! [*To the audience*] Ladies and gentlemen, a slight pause before my son returns.

In the meantime the blind children would adore it if
they saw you reaching even further into your pockets.
Our target tonight is five hundred pounds, so dip your
hands in. Go on, the heavens are clear and fortune
shines on us tonight.

SCENE EIGHTEEN

The wilds of south-western Tasmania, day. FRANCIS *lies on
the ground, dirty and sleepy. There is a sudden noise and he
wakes up.* PETER *appears wearing his old hiking gear.*
FRANCIS *is surprised to see his friend. Silence.*

PETER: I knew you'd come back here.
FRANCIS: Are there any others with you?
PETER: No.
   [*Pause.*]
  Are you all right?
FRANCIS: Tired, that's all.
PETER: I'm not used to all this exercise.
FRANCIS: [*smiling*] Neither am I.
   [*Silence.*]
PETER: Betsheb?
FRANCIS: Down by the river.
PETER: When I got to the asylum, Doctor Simon was still
  shaking. She said you were about to shoot Betsheb and
  when she called out you turned the gun on her.
FRANCIS: I wanted to put Betsheb out of her misery, but
  when I held it against her head I realised I should have
  been holding it against mine. I knew what to do. I
  would bring Betsheb back here, bring her home. We
  destroyed them.
PETER: It was a combination of events. How were we to
  know that the Government would deal with them that
  way?
FRANCIS: Does it bother you?
PETER: It does, but I have never been obsessed by them

as you are or my father was. How could they have
survived, anyway? They were pathetic remnants of
what was probably an even more pathetic collection of
people. They were like those Aboriginal tribes that
withered away because their culture wasn't strong
enough. It happens in nature, in human civilisations,
one big animal swallows a little one. [*Looking around*]
It didn't take long for it to return to the wilderness.

> [BETSHEB *enters and smiles when she sees* PETER. *She
> hugs him.*]

BETSHEB: Peter, Peter, Peter.

PETER: Hello, Betsheb. [*To* FRANCIS] Are you going to
stay here ... with her?

FRANCIS: Why not?

> [*He releases* BETSHEB, *and she lies on the ground and
> stares contentedly at the sky.*]

PETER: You're mad. How in hell will you two survive out
here?

FRANCIS: They survived; why not us? It doesn't matter,
anyway. Why should I go back? How can I go back
after all I've seen? This is what I hate about this
country: it pretends nothing important ever
happened. Everything we experienced overseas ... we
return and pretend we never experienced it. I shot
that German, not out of pity, but because I was filled
with hate. All right, pretend it didn't happen. You
helped co-ordinate the bombing raids over Germany.
Forget it. We obliterated a group of people, not
through deliberate cruelty, but through plain
stupidity and indifference. Doesn't matter, no
problems, mate. Indifference is our guiding star. We'd
sooner turn our attention to making a quick quid, like
children amused by shiny trinkets. We'd sooner wipe
out all unpleasant memories, block our ears and
pretend we can't hear the cry of pain. If we heard that
cry, then our sense of ourselves would be deeper, then
we shall have reached home. We are lost, rootless
people: she isn't.

PETER: You're running away.

> [*Silence.*]

FRANCIS: Will you stay with us for tonight?

PETER: If I leave now, I'll get back to the track before dark.

[*Pause.*]

I'll say I couldn't find you.

[*He looks at* BETSHEB, *who still lies on the ground staring contentedly up at the sky and trees.*]

BETSHEB: [*happily*] Rack 'n' cat o' the windy, bumpin' thru the trees.

PETER: She can't offer you a future.

BETSHEB: Sprits o' Melorne, Ayre, Stef, Mac, Angel. Liptalkin' softly, swirlin' in the cunty dell o' moss 'n' ferny clotty 'eart. The moon is a white 'ole, I crawl int' it t' dream. Ayre liptalkin' thru me 'eart. The bird listen, he liptalk thru 'is soul. Sprits outburstin' around 'n' around, a-yellin, a-kissin'. All goldy things. All goldy sow. 'Ome. I come 'ome.

[*Silence.*]

PETER: What she's describing doesn't exist; it's a figment of her imagination.

FRANCIS: She can teach me how to see it.

PETER: But it's not real.

BETSHEB: [*softly, singing*]

> Rain, rain, go thy way,
> Come a-back ne'er a day.

PETER: Goodbye, Betsheb.

[*She pays no attention.*]

She lives in a world of her own. You know that. She destroyed my father just as she'll destroy you. You have done the wrong thing.

FRANCIS: Maybe I have; I don't know. But she's all I've got to believe in.

PETER: Goodbye.

[FRANCIS *nods a 'Goodbye.'* PETER *departs. Silence.* BETSHEB *continues to sing softly to herself.*]

FRANCIS: Betsheb? Betsheb?

[BETSHEB, *immersed in her own world, doesn't answer.* FRANCIS *sits down away from her and wonders if* PETER *is right.* BETSHEB *laughs to herself. After a time she turns around and notices* FRANCIS: *a lonely, confused figure. She stares at him and, almost as if he has heard his name, he turns and looks at her. She smiles across the gulf that separates them.*]

BETSHEB: Nowt more outcastin'.

[*The lights fade slowly to blackout.*]

THE END.

GLOSSARY

12 AYRE To the greeny pallor o' thee kingspot; o' cunty goldy. ['*Welcome to this green land fit for kings, this land rich and fertile.*']

13 AYRE: [*smiling*] I bunter t' the windy sheet, t' the arsemine o' the world. Breathe a vein, breathe a vein. [*Shaking her head*] Olcers an' 'ellpain. [*Tapping her chair*] Starry, shiny, cunty dell o' me world. ['*I sometimes feel I am fluttering in the wind, or other times I am at the bottom of the world. Have a rest, take it easy. Ulcers and hellish pain. This chair is the shining centre of my world.*']

   MELORNE: [*thickly*] Fer skilly we gobble in awe. ['*For this food we thank you and will eat it with the proper respect.*']

14 AYRE: Born o' cat 'n' rack 'n' goldy sow. ['*He was born of a past that included both prisoners who remembered the cat-o-nine-tails and the rack and fertile gold mines.*']
   He fed on tarse o' dark in the black quim o' a belle. ['*He was fed by a diseased penis while he was in the diseased womb of a young girl.*']
   Skittle. Skittle. Blackfortune. ['*It was chance. Chance. Misfortune.*']

15 AYRE:

> In the night,
> In the day,
> Blue ruins, blue ruins
> In Jack's Inn Bay.
> ['*In the night,*
> *In the day,*
> *Drinking blue ruin, blue ruin*
> *Travelling towards Jackson's Bay.*]

MELORNE: Bleak street o' fen 'n' bellies. Dark trees 'n' no trees betide bleak sand. ['*Bleak landscape of ferns and valleys. There are also dark woods and places with no trees down near the ocean.*']
'Toady o' the holy! Bleak King o' the dark. Thou walk on loam cooked o' thou disease. Thou disease pox on the land in blood 'n' pig. [*Indicating the land and sky*] 'Rye o' the sky, rye o' the loam. Morn 'n' dark all topsy turvy.' [*Motioning to himself*] 'I, King. King o' cits.' [*Crying out*] 'Trellion! Trellion!' ['"*Poisonous toad. King of Darkness. You walk on the soil that is made warm by your corruption and disease. You have diseased this country; it smells like pig and bone. The fertile sky, the fertile soil. The rich sky and soil is now diseased, everything is upside-down, darkness is morning, morning is darkness. I am King. King of all citizens. Rebellion and treason! Rebellion and treason!*"']
MELORNE: 'A lik a lik a lik a lik a lik ...' ['"*I lick I lick I lick I lick I lick ...*"']

16 AYRE: 'Poor quim me am, bleak father. Forgive me, bleak father. The 'eaven is wild. Torn athunder so bad, so bad, we fain to live.' ['"*I am a poor empty womb, stern Father. Forgive me, stern Father. The heavens are so wild, so violent that we are afraid to live.*"']
MELORNE: [*yelling*] 'Ye child, dry quim. Ye rack o' truth I boil, this loam boil 'cos o' me profoundest outcastin'. [*With high emotion*] 'Outcastin'!' [*Crying at the sky*] 'Rack 'n' cat, rack 'n' cat!' ['"*You child, you have a dry cunt. I am racked by the truth of it all. I am upset, the soil is upset, because I am in exile. Exiled! The sky sounds like whipping!*"']
'Ye blind! Ye blind! Now, foresooth, ye can eye me pain o' outcastin'. Ye pain goldy sow o' me tarse!' ['"*You are blind. Only now can you see the pain I feel at my exile. You are the corrupted sperm of my cock.*"']
MELORNE: [*as though in his second childhood*] 'Bleak outcastin', a blub, blub, blub.' ['"*Terrible exile, a blub, blub, blub.*"']

'True treasure o' quim 'n' tarse! ['*Honest fruit of womb and cock!*"']
'Nowt more outcastin'! Nowt more!' ['*No more exile! No more!*"']
'Joyful quim! Joyful tarse! Joyful bird! Joyful goldy sow! Joyful day!' ['*Joyful womb! Joyful cock! Joyful bird! Joyful gold mine! Joyful day!*"']
'Joy o' loam.' [*Quietly*] 'Nowt more outcastin! Nowt more.' ['*Joyful soil. No more exile! No more.*"']

18 AYRE: 'O tell me, bird, t' where is yer goin'? O tell me, what is yer want t' hear?' [*Smiling at the two men*] New chums. Skittle o' chance has yer to this spot, here, down in a fine ol' dark. [*'You're new arrivals. Chance and accident has brought you to this spot, this place hidden deep in the country.'*]
I cup me ear t' the glommen bird. Soul o' the dead. Cryin' out, 'Donna burst er 'eart, the bird is me!' No rack'n' cat. Heavenbirth. [*'I listen to the night bird. He is the soul of the dead. He is singing to me, 'Don't be alarmed, I am what is singing.' The bird is no demon. Born in heaven.'*]
Me, moonin' in the glommen. [*'Look at me, saying silly things to the night.'*]
[*With an all-encompassing motion of her hands*] Our .igoldy sow, the furst t' bloodburst int' this silent sea. Past riverrun 'n' turn o' kelp int' muddy moss, seay green 'n' here. 'Ere! Sprit eyes o' gold. In ghost time, behind us; osier 'n' 'eather 'n' 'ello, ducky. 'Oary boyos, sun-stricken girlie days. Blackysmith 'n' Trunk's Tavern. I hear the goldy lifey, the glommen lifey. Do nowt ferget dreamytime. Ferget lifey in rattlesnake, ev'ry chum cryin' to death, 'n' into 'ere, the greeny belch o' 'eaven. Danderupping so to live on the greasypole o' sprit friends. Sprits o' cunty dell. Circle o' greeny 'ome. Stars 'n' loam, firs 'n' spermy flower. Sprits, sprits, ghosts 'n' pitch dark, buboes o' the face 'n' arse 'n' ... 'n' festerin' lip 'n' baby birdcry. Burst mouth, hairy brain 'n' cradlepain. Goldy death,

goldy backward seein'. [*Motioning to her head*] Me mossy brain is the backward seein'. Pitch dark glommen is dry sheb and rottin' tarse. The circle is burst. [*Softly, almost to herself*] The circle is burst. [*'Our ancestors were the first to venture into this wilderness. They came over rivers, through seas, through mud and slush, thick woods to reach here. Here! Here we saw flecks of gold. In the past, the past of our ancestors, there were osier and heather and people said 'Hello, ducky.' There were also randy boys and sun-filled, girl-filled days. There were blacksmiths and Trunk's Tavern. I listened to stories of the golden life in the past and also the darkness of the past (or the dark life). I was told not to forget my past dream-life in England. I was told to forget life in the prison ships, where every prisoner cried until they died. Then we reached here: the green stomach of heaven. But you had to get your dander up, be prepared, full of energy if you lived in this place because of all the spirits. It is like living on a greasy pole, always on guard, nothing certain. We call them the spirits of this fertile valley. This circle of greenery we call home. Home is stars and rich soil, fir trees and fertile flowers. Spirits and the mischievous, even deadly spirits; but there are also ghosts and deep darkness, blisters and boils which grow on the face and arse, and there are hare lips and babies which, because of this, can only make bird cries. There are also cleft palates, useless brains and babies born in pain. Death can be good, as can looking into the past. My old brain contains the past. Do you know what true, deep darkness is? It's sterile cunts and useless pricks. Everything is broken. Everything is broken.'*]
[*Looking at the sky*] I cup me ear t' the glommen bird.
  [*'I like to listen to the nightbird.'*]

24 BETSHEB: [*to* FRANCIS, *with a very thick accent*] Stef 'ave cradlepain. [*'Stef was born diseased.'*]

26 BETSHEB: [*murmuring softly*]

        Rain, rain, go thy way,

Come a back ne'er a day ...
['*Rain, rain, go away,*
Come back again another day ...']

AYRE: 'airloomin' fer the child. Wot child? Bellsademon
laughin'. Nowt need nowt Herrod. We is dead. Goldy
dead nowt goldy sow. Nowt tongue, nowt goldy sow,
nowt 'istory. ['*This would have been an heirloom for the
child. But what child? The devils are laughing at me. We
don't need King Herod (to kill our children). We are dead.
The gold mine is finished, there is no fertile womb or sperm.
We have no language, no sperm, and therefore no history.*']
So fine. So fine. 'I shew yer beauty. Beauty so fine yer'll
piss yerself. 'airloomin' fer the child.' ['*So beautiful. So
beautiful. "I'll show you beauty, beauty so wonderful that
you'll piss yourself. An heirloom for the child."*']
Nowt more outcastin'. [*Crying out to the sky*] Nowt more
outcastin'! ['*No more exile. No more exile.*']

27 BETSHEB: [*pretending to read, turning the pages quickly*]
Thy word. ['*This is your book.*']
'ate the olcer sky. No end. No end. Adorate the shiny
brocade sky, glommen time. Queenie Ayre say in
ancient glommen, King David see the brocade, King
Moses see the goldy brocade, lubilashings o' shiny in
ancient glommen. The sky 'e see, is me goldy brocade.
See? ['*I hate the sky when it looks dark and threatening.
There seems to be no end to darkness when it's like that. No
end. I adore the shiny, starry sky at night. Queenie Ayre says
that back in the old times, King David saw the shiny, starry
sky; King Moses also saw the golden stars. There were
incredible numbers of stars back in ancient times. The sky
they saw is the same golden starry sky I see.*']

28 BETSHEB: Me burstin' brain. Me burstin' brain. See? ['*My
head feels like it's exploding. My head feels like it's
exploding. See?*']
BETSHEB: Break 'n' crack int' thee. ['*I want to crack and
break your skull and get directly through to you.*']

30 BETSHEB: Bellsademon kissin' 'n' spoonkissin' in the rye.
     [*Murmering*] The belle she lie droopin'. The gent he lie
     tongue out. Ho! Spoonfuckin' in the glommen. [*'Let's
     kiss like demons and put our tongues down each other's
     mouths while we're here in the grass. The woman lies ready,
     the boy has his tongue out. Ho! Fucking in the night.'*]
     BETSHEB: [*smiling, softly*] The belle whoopin', tongue out
     in the glommen. [*'The girl is randy, she has her tongue out
     in the night.'*]

32 AYRE: [*to* FRANCIS *and* PETER] The circle is burst. We is
     burstin' int' the glommen. Outburst. Bellsademon
     land; cradlepain. Circle is burst. Nowt more
     outcastin'. Nowt more sin fer bread. [*'Everything has
     broken apart. We are breaking apart into the night.
     Exploding outwards. This land is the Devil's land, full of
     awful pain. No more exile, but no more prostituting
     ourselves as in the old days either.'*]
     Goldy sow o' the 'airloomin' pit. [*'In this box are all the
     best things, the heirlooms.'*]
     Sa, Sa. [*'Sarah, Sarah.'*]
     Promin'. 'Airloomin'. [*'For promenading. It's an
     heirloom.'*]

36 BETSHEB: [*quietly*] The belle is spoonin'. [*'The girl is
     happy.'*]

46 AYRE'S VOICE: Past riverrun 'n' turn o' kelp int' muddy
     moss, seay green 'n' here. There! Ghost 'n' sprit time.
     Goldy lifey, glommen lifey. Thee dreamytime in
     greeny belch o' 'eaven. Sprits o' cunty dell. Circle o'
     greeny 'ome! Nowt 'ome. Burst mouth, hairy brain 'n'
     cradlepain. Pitch dark glommen is dry sheb and rottin'
     tarse. The circle is burst ... [*'They came over rivers,
     through seas, through mud and slush, thick woods to reach
     there. There! It was a time of ghosts and wicked spirits. Life
     in the past was golden, but also dark. The past dream-life
     in the green stomach of heaven. The wicked spirits of this
     fertile valley. This circle of greenery we call home! But it's*

*not home. There were cleft palates, useless brains and babies
born in pain. True, deep darkness is sterile cunts and
useless pricks. Everything is broken ...'*]

48 BETSHEB: I ear op'n t' the Angel sprit. ['*I hear the spirt of
Angel.*']
BETSHEB: Lorry. Gard-aner.
['*Larry.*']
BETSHEB: This dress? Nowt dirt. Me weddon dress. [*'This
dress? I won't dirty it. It's my wedding dress.'*]

49 BETSHEB: There. Our bedibyes. Glommen time. [*'There.
Going to bed. Night-time.'*
BETSHEB: There is a man, he listens, speakin' t' glommen
demon. This girl ... ['*There is a man, he listens and speaks
to the night demon ...'*]
BETSHEB: I 'ate glommen time 'ere. 'Eads burst,
outburstin' wid demons. ['*I hate night-time here. Heads
explode and break open and send forth demons.'*
BETSHEB: Me quim is burnin'. ['*I'm randy.'*]
BETSHEB: [*moving to him again*] Thou burning. Eyebright.
['*You're randy too. Your eyes are bright with lust.'*]
BETSHEB: The belle she spoonin' the gent. He whoopin'.
[*The girl is lusting after the man. He is happy.*]

51 BETSHEB: Nowt 'Goodbye'. ['*Don't say "Goodbye".'*]
AYRE: Demon 'ollarin' in glommen time. ['*Demons yell in
the night.'*]
AYRE: Sprits o' rack 'n' cat, doomtime.' ['*When the spirits
make sounds like a rack and cat, it means someone is
doomed.'*]
AYRE: Sprits adorate quim sold for sinbread. [*'Spirits like
prostitutes.'*]
AYRE: Albion is glommentime, rack 'n' cat time.
['*England is full of night; it was a time of whippings, rack
and cat.'*]

52 AYRE: Glommen sprits o' cut-throat kin. [*'Night spirits are
related to our violent ancestors, the true criminals.'*]

AYRE: Pass 'elly gate t' goldy dell. [*We passed through hell's gate to get to the golden valley.*']

AYRE: [*to* BETSHEB] Pearly dawn pass glommen time, thou pass demon time. Pass tempest 'n' temper time. [*If you can survive night-time, then dawn will come and you will have survived another night of demons and the wilds and anger of nature.*']

56   BETSHEB: Goldy green breathen int' thee, rain breathen int' thee. [*Nature is breathing into you, the rain is breathing into you.*']

BETSHEB: The earth breathen int' thee. Thou mus' live! [*'The earth breathes into you. You must live!*']

BETSHEB: [*breathing into* AYRE'*s mouth*] I am in thee, thee in me. [*Thumping* AYRE] Breathen! Breathen the tempest! Breathen the rain! [*Crying out, desperately*] Breathen the world! Thee must breathen the world! [*'I am in you, you in me. Breathe! Breathe in the rain! Breathe in the world! You must breathe in the world!*'

BETSHEB: Breathen! Breathen the world! The world is breathen thee! Mumma! Breathen! [*'Breathe! Breathe in the world! The world is breathing you! Mumma! Breathe!*']

57   BETSHEB: Pass snow; nowt more outcastin'. [*'Once it has finished snowing, his exile will be over.*']

58   BETSHEB: The belly o' 'er quim. Lovely. [*'Her belly is full. It's lovely.*']

BETSHEB: Francis outcastin'; come back 'n' look at 'is belle 'n' 'e think 'the dead moon o' me cunt.' [*'Francis is in exile, but when he comes back and looks at his girl he will think that I have a dead moon in my cunt.*']

BETSHEB: Me bod shakin' like a leaf, out o' the blue. [*'My body shakes like a leaf; these attacks come on suddenly.*']

BETSHEB: Me bod in the toothy bite o' a bad dream. [*'My body is in the toothy bite of a bad dream.*']

62   BETSHEB: 'e me las' blood. Stef is me las' blood. I am cast t' the windy. He me las' blood boyo. [*'Stef is my last*

relative, the last of my family. I am cast adrift. He was the last male member of the family.

67 BETSHEB: [*screaming*] Nowt more! ['*No more!*']

76 BETSHEB: [*happily*] Rack 'n' cat o' the windy, bumpin' thru the trees. ['*The wind sounds like the rack and cat as it blows through the trees.*'

BETSHEB: Sprits o' Melorne, Ayre, Stef, Mac, Angel. Liptalkin' softly, swirlin' in the cunty dell o' moss 'n' ferny clotty 'eart. The moon is a white 'ole, I crawl int' it t' dream. Ayre liptalkin' thru me 'eart. The bird listen, he liptalk thru 'is soul. Sprits outburstin' around 'n' around, a-yellin, a-kissin'. All goldy things. All goldy sow. 'Ome. I come 'ome. ['*I can hear the spirits of Melorne, Ayre, Stef, Mac and Angel talking softly. I hear their voices swirling down through the valley and up through the mosses and ferns, so thick they are like a fern-clotted heart. The moon is like a white hole; I crawl into it when I dream. Ayre is speaking through my heart. The night-bird listens, but when he talks he talks through his soul. Spirits are bursting out and dancing around, yelling and kissing. Everything is fertile, wonderful. Home. I have come home.*']

77 BETSHEB: Nowt more outcastin'. ['*No more exile.*']

For a full list of our titles, visit our website:

www.currency.com.au

Currency Press
The performing arts publisher
PO Box 2287
Strawberry Hills NSW 2012
Australia
enquiries@currency.com.au
Tel: (02) 9319 5877
Fax: (02) 9319 3649